"The prison system is one of those forgotten places where the shadow of the culture reigns and needs to be brought to light and to humanitarian enlightenment. Thanks for your work."

Anodea Judith, Ph.D.
Author of *Waking the Global Heart and Wheels of Life*

"I applaud Veronica Shaffer's courage and commitment, and her dedication to bring the wisdom she has earned on her own spiritual journey to the prison community."

Elizabeth K. Stratton, M.S.
Author of *Touching Spirit and Seeds of Light*

"I Hear You Cry is an inspiring story of empowerment that describes the use of Eastern spiritual techniques in the unlikely setting of a women's prison. Veronica Shaffer has done good work, not only in bringing contemplative practices to a population in need, but also in telling us this compelling story. I commend her."

Eric Leskowitz MD, Director, Integrative Medicine Project
Spaulding Rehabilitation Hospital
Department of Psychiatry, Harvard Medical School

"This book reveals the manner in which any Being can step outside of the mind's prison."

Venerable Dhyani Ywahoo, Spiritual Leader and Peacemaker
Author of *Voice of Our Ancestors*

I Hear Your Cry:
Women in Prison

I Hear Your Cry:
Women in Prison

Veronica A. Shaffer

iUniverse, Inc.
New York Lincoln Shanghai

I Hear Your Cry: Women in Prison

iUniverse books may be ordered through booksellers or by contacting:

iUniverse
2021 Pine Lake Road, Suite 100
Lincoln, NE 68512
www.iuniverse.com
1-800-Authors (1-800-288-4677)

This book is non-fiction and is based on my experiences teaching yoga
and meditation to women in prison. Teaching in prison has been one of
the most fulfilling experiences of my life, however, to protect the true
identities and privacy of all the individuals I encountered in my work in
the prison system, I have changed the names and distinguishing
characteristics of the inmates and prison officials, as well as my family
members. Some of the events described happened as related, others were
expanded and changed. Some of the individuals portrayed are composites
of more than one person.

Library of Congress Registration Number:
TXu1-319-824

Photographer: Mark Howell

Cover Design: Ray Palmer IV

ISBN-13: 978-0-595-40563-3 (pbk)
ISBN-13: 978-0-595-84928-4 (ebk)
ISBN-10: 0-595-40563-0 (pbk)
ISBN-10: 0-595-84928-8 (ebk)

Printed in the United States of America

This book is dedicated to my husband, Edward and my children, Kathy, Ray III and Alan.

Without you, I would not have learned the lessons nor received the loving support that allowed me to bring this story to fruition. For this, I honor you.

May we continue to grow on our journey together.

Acknowledgements

My greatest debt is to the women in prison with whom I have had an opportunity to work. Without these women, there would be no story and an important part of my own healing process might not have taken place.

Special recognition to my first program director who recognized that the type of fitness and wellness program I offered had the potential to initiate positive changes in prisoners. I am equally grateful to my second program director, who obtained permission for us to use yoga mats after two years on a hard concrete floor. She also recognized the importance of accepting books for the units, and was always willing to work with me to keep improving the program and making my schedule consistent.

To Pam Summa, my writing coach, I offer deep gratitude for her belief in my ability to write and in the worthiness of the story, even when I wasn't sure I believed in myself.

Linda Hewitt, my editor, who took my many pieces of paper and made them into well defined chapters, helping me shape the manuscript into the story I wanted to tell. Thank you for listening and hearing my story.

Pauline Stieff, who did much research into agents and publishers and spent many hours honing my computer skills to make this an ideal manuscript. I am thankful for the times we've spent together both as a colleague and friend.

To Joan Foley, I am appreciative of your superb manuscript preparation, always completed before the deadline.

Beth David, my copy editor, your grammar review was invaluable. Thanks for those last minute phone calls to fill in the gaps in preparation for the publisher.

My personal life has been blessed with many who believed in and supported me, especially my husband, Edward Shaffer, who offered excellent suggestions and read and re-read while I typed long past midnight.

Warm thanks to dear friends, Dr. Betsy Drucker, whose suggestions and opinions in reading my manuscript were key to its completion. Dr. Edna Hamilton, whose friendship helped brighten some of my single years in preparation for my story. Dr. Tina Poussaint, who pushed me forward when I was lagging behind, and Dr. Alvin Poussaint, for your recommendations, I am grateful.

Billie Jo Joy deserves recognition for reading the manuscript as I valued her input.

My sister, Rose, whose vivid memories filled in some of the events I had not always wanted to be reminded of.

Richard Allen, my dear friend and therapist, helped me heal my heart through his insight and counseling. Through our work together, I have gained a better understanding of love in whatever form it appears.

To all those who have heard my story and supported my many years of working on this book, I am deeply indebted.

Contents

Foreword xv

Part I *The Journey*

Introduction 3

Orientation 13

First Class 18

The Tibetan Bells 29

Being the Stranger 36

Christmas and the Full Moon 40

Peter Becomes an Ally 47

Hear Our Voices 53

Sliding into the Next Session 56

Part II *The Women*

Prelude 71

Sui 73

Cecily 79

Meet the Pregnant Mamas 83

Luvell 87

Atlanta 93

Ebony 96

Mimie 98

A New Perspective on a Haunting Memory 100

Part III   Transition

And Then There Was Change 107

Last Class Before Going Inside the Recovery Unit 113

Inside the Recovery Unit 117

Monthly Canteen 122

Holiday in the Recovery Unit 126

Therapy 133

Graduation 136

The Reunion 141

Part IV   A New Design

A Different Approach 147

Colors and Numbers 151

The Holding Pattern 155

The Revolving Door 161

Celebration and Commitment 165

A Final Note to the Reader 173

Foreword

Why did I write about women in prison?

Each one of those women represented a piece of me. I may not have been incarcerated, but I had periods in my life when I felt I was *imprisoned*.

I was married to an alcoholic and had three young children. No money. My family lived out of state, no support system. I felt powerless and desperate. I drew on my spiritual strength to get through the hard times. I drew on the unconditional love from my little ones to wake up every day, working two jobs to support them. Survive—will I? Survive—I must!

Working in the recovery unit with the women brought back those memories of late-night drunken episodes; no job, no money. The tears and broken promises, wanting to believe he'll change until the next drunken binge. My visits to Al-Anon, AA and psychotherapy. A long road to recovery, a never-ending journey. A piece of history in each one of those women.

I identified with their struggles to get out of prison only to be drawn back in prison.

I drew on the strength from my soul, my spirit. The will to succeed.

It was one step at a time, one moment, one minute, and slowly the tide began to change.

A few steps forward, then a step back, but I continued to pull the rope to freedom. "Hold on for your life."

These were experiences of a lifetime that I brought to those women. Listening to their stories, which part was me? Luvell, pregnant in jail. That's how I felt when I became pregnant with my third child, trapped. Cecily, wanting to be loved and made to feel safe. That part of me that never felt genuinely loved as a child and wife. Sui, exploring the world of drugs with a questionable boyfriend. I kissed a lot of frogs before I found *my prince.*

Some of the women change while incarcerated, and some do not. What did I mirror to those women as I taught my program? What pieces of myself have I healed, and what pieces of myself need healing?

PART I
The Journey

Introduction

As I stood on my deck one fall morning five years ago, I watched the gentle movement of the Tibetan prayer flags that I had tied between two of my tall pine trees. Watching these flags blow in the breeze comforted me.

I first saw them on a trip to Tibet seven years ago. Wherever I traveled, I noticed these colorful prayer flags hanging from the roofs of temples, monasteries and mountains. Sometimes they were hung between poles. I felt amazed at how many blew in the breeze as trekkers climbed toward Mount Everest.

Each vivid square is inscribed with a prayer. Blue represents space, white is water, red represents fire, green is for air, and yellow for earth. Tibetans believe that hanging prayer flags with intention releases positive energized blessings out to the world on the wind, spreading these blessings to all beings and assisting those who hang the flags. These prayer flags flutter in all kinds of weather. Some days they move softly in a light breeze; on other days, a strong wind sends their prayers surging outward to the world.

On that fall morning, at home, I felt transported to a peaceful place—one I don't often experience. Calmness fell over me, and my inner voice whispered that I needed to share some of the teachings I had received over the years. I found myself nodding in agreement as though I were having a conversation with someone.

At certain times in my life, this same inner voice has guided me through life-altering moments. One of the most important moments of this kind was in the mid-sixties, when I decided to go home to

Pennsylvania for Thanksgiving and spend time with my family. Flying had just become popular as a timesaving alternative to driving, so I made plane reservations for my three children—ages two, four and five—and me. I was excited to spend the holiday with my parents and six younger siblings.

I felt trapped in my marriage at the time, and this was an opportunity to talk with my mother about my unhappiness. Perhaps time and distance would help me decide to escape an unhealthy environment. I knew I was at a crossroads, and Brad's drinking was out of control. He couldn't hold a job, and what money he earned mostly went toward supporting the local pub.

After making the airline reservations, I spent the rest of the afternoon packing. I even found myself humming as I gathered the laundry and wrote a list of necessary items to take on the trip. Packing for myself was easy, but three small children needed everything from diapers to winter gear, and play clothes to holiday bests. I could already smell the turkey cooking in the kitchen and imagined my mother up early making pie crusts, filling them with fresh mincemeat and pumpkin. I would be free, if just for a few days.

That night, after the family was tucked into bed, I checked my list to make sure I hadn't missed anything and finally went to bed myself. As soon as I settled my head on the soft, white pillow, I envisioned a plane crash. I saw myself in a field standing by a fence, terrified because I couldn't find my children. Looking up at the dark sky, I heard an inner voice speak to me.

"You can't fly," the voice said. "There will be no children if you do."

Shaken, I jumped out of bed, ran to the bathroom, and got a drink of water. I shook my head as if it would clear away what I had seen and heard, but again the voice warned me not to fly home. I took two aspirins and went back to bed, hoping the pills would relieve me of the sights and sounds I had just witnessed. I fell into a deep sleep and awoke in the early morning to the sound of my youngest crying to get out of bed.

I knew I had to change my travel plans and go to Pennsylvania by train. The difference in travel time was seven hours, but I didn't hesitate as I told my husband that I was changing our reservations. I explained excitedly what had happened to me the previous night.

"You're crazy. It was just a bad dream, but do what you want," Brad said, just as I'd expected.

When I called my mother to tell her about the dream and let her know I would arrive by train, she did not respond. I was thankful for her silence. I began to feel better and more peaceful. No matter what my husband thought, I knew I was doing the right thing.

The day before Thanksgiving, I gathered the suitcases and the children, and left on a snowy morning's drive to Boston's South Station. My husband, who was driving, preferred sports talk to music, so he had the radio on the news station.

A news flash then announced that the flight I had been scheduled to take with my children had crashed, and there were no survivors. I wasn't surprised. Brad turned and looked at me with such amazement that he almost drove off the expressway into the guardrail.

"I told you!" I remembered saying firmly.

My mother, brother Frank, and sister Mary greeted us in the small, dismal Pennsylvania train station. There was one ticket agent, and you usually carried your own luggage off the train unless there was a conductor standing by the steps. If he saw you struggling, he might offer his assistance.

"You had better go see Jean Dixon," Mary said as my family embraced the children.

She was referring to the then-famous Washington astrologer and psychic. I smiled with gratitude.

My visit was relaxing, and I savored every minute. I called a few of my high school friends, and they dropped by; we exchanged current news about our former classmates and compared notes about our babies.

I never seemed to find the right time to be alone with my mother. Perhaps I was holding back, fearful of what she would say, or maybe I felt guilty about having made the wrong choice in a marriage partner. I didn't want to hear, "I told you so." My trip home did not provide answers for my deepening despair.

As my life continued to unravel, I wanted desperately to hear my inner voice direct my life, but it didn't speak to me again until many years later when I met my present husband for the first time.

Greeting him at the door of my apartment, I shook his hand, and I immediately felt safe.

"You're going to marry him," the voice said.

He's nice," I thought, "but not my type."

I had usually dated heavier, more muscular men, and Ed wasn't either. He wore a topcoat for the March weather, and I thought he looked thin even with all that padding. When we were dating, I continually heard the inner message about marrying him.

"Pay attention to his honesty and compassion and the love he has for people," the voice urged.

These little reminders directed me to be aware of his inner qualities and not the physical characteristics I had so often looked for in my male companions. Twenty-two years later, still happily married, I'm grateful that I listened to my inner voice.

◆   ◆   ◆

Most of my adult years, I worked in hospitals as a radiological technologist. Years of lifting patients and moving portable X-ray machines through the hospital had weakened my neck and back. Medications weren't working, so I sought help elsewhere and became involved in alternative medicine, seeking ways to build a healthy body. When I was fifty-five, I injured my back and neck so severely that I was unable to continue working in the hospital. My orthopedic physician advised me to stay as active as possible so that my body would not atrophy. I studied yoga and felt so pleased with the results that I decided to take a teacher certification.

I chose to study with superb teachers in Princeton, Massachusetts. The twice-monthly, all-day Saturdays fit nicely into my schedule. I had a friend, Susan, who shared the hour-and-a-half drive with me, so it was manageable. This training lasted nine months. When I graduated, I knew that I, as well as others, would benefit from what I had learned.

For this reason, I began wondering about what type of volunteer service I could perform in the community. By sharing with injured people the postures that had helped me, I thought perhaps I could enhance their lives. I had earned my yoga certification and led meditation groups in my home twice a month. The combination of the two modalities improved my well-being, and my students began to respond positively. Maybe I could teach a monthly meditation and yoga class at our community center.

"Yes," I thought, and suddenly my inner voice suggested that I work with women in prison. I felt my face light up. I began to feel energized. Prisons had always intrigued me. Some people have described me as someone who lives on the edge, or, as my daughter Catherine likes to say, "loves an adventure." My son John calls me Joan of Arc. I thought I fit the profile for this type of work.

◆　　　◆　　　◆

Perhaps another factor that pulled me toward working in prison was what had happened to my grandson, Michael. He had been incarcerated, and the thought of a similar incident in my family recurring was painful to me. He was fourteen years old when he and a friend decided to skip school, take the family car, and go on a joy ride, which began in Wisconsin. In Alabama, Michael and Andrew realized they needed more gas. Out of money and with no charge cards or bank accounts, they stopped at a gas station, pumped $2 worth, and took off without paying. The attendant was livid. He called the local police, and the chase began.

The boys were scared; driving recklessly, they hoped to outrun the police. In the wild pursuit, they crossed over into Florida, the cops hot on their trail. Then Michael hit a construction worker, who was directing traffic, head on. The impact caused the construction worker to go through the windshield and severed his head from his body. The chase was over, and lives were instantly changed forever. A wife lost her husband and a two-year-old girl lost her daddy. Two teenagers were off to a Florida prison for several years, removed from the safety of home and family.

My first introduction to prison was the juvenile facility where my daughter Catherine and I visited Michael. As we drove up to the main gate of the prison in the Florida Panhandle, I was surprised to see perfectly manicured lawns and a few palm trees surrounding the facility. The only thing that reminded me that this was a jail was a high, barbed-wire fence in the back of the building. There was no lookout tower with an officer watching the yard, as in movie prisons.

When we entered the lobby, a friendly receptionist asked us for identification and directed us to the waiting room. As we walked the halls, I noticed that the interior of the facility resembled that of an office complex, with many offices buzzing with telephones and computers. I saw no bars on the windows and no prison officers. Several pictures of past sheriffs decorated the walls. I began to imagine that their eyes were watching my every move.

Michael arrived with his counselor, a young woman in her late twenties. Catherine and I stood up as Michael rushed toward us. All three of us embraced in a bear hug. I wondered if the counselor had a teenage brother or someone close whom she could imagine in Michael's situation.

"I'm Tara," she said, as she shook hands.

"I'm Catherine, Michael's mother," my daughter said. She nodded toward me. "This is Michael's grandmother, Mrs. Shaffer."

Tara turned to Catherine. "Has there been any other trouble with Michael before this incident?"

"He'd been on medication for the past two years to control his aggressive behavior. He hung with schoolmates who were in and out of trouble, and his father and I were concerned. We ordered him to cut the ties, but he wouldn't listen," Catherine answered in tears, her voice cracking.

As Michael and his mother embraced again, tears ran down their cheeks. We hadn't seen him in three months. I felt my throat tighten and my own tears welling as his counselor led us to her office for more general questions about family history and Michael's childhood. Catherine shared with Tara that she had given birth to Michael at age sixteen, a natural birth.

"He was an easy baby, and he formed a strong attachment to his father at an early age," she continued. "I had finished high school and then started studying to become a nurse. I was totally caught up in my studies, so Greg spent a lot of time with Michael—feeding him, changing diapers and responding to late-night cries."

I sat back and listened to her responses, feeling the heaviness in my heart as I recalled the innocence of his baby years.

Tara explained that we would have five hours to visit that day, which was Saturday, and four hours on Sunday. I felt grateful for the time we would have alone and was anxious to hear Michael's tales of incarceration.

Catherine and I were escorted to a ball field that was part of the facility, and we waited for a prison guard to arrive with Michael. We had no place to sit except for the seats in our rental car or on the ground, and there was a chill in the air, so when Michael got there, we spent most of our time together in the car, turning the heat on intermittently. Catherine and I showed Michael photographs of the family, wanting him to see the love and support that was there for him. We had pictures of the different stages of his fourteen years, and we laughed and reminisced. When he looked at a photo of his grandfather, who had passed away six months before, he started to cry. Again I held back my tears. Michael was the oldest grandchild, and he held a special place in *Papa's* heart.

As I write about Michael today, recalling that scene fills me with grief. I am surprised that I still react so emotionally to events of so long ago.

An odd memory from that weekend was driving to McDonald's to bring back a lunch of burgers and fries and not being searched upon my return. I never expected a prison visitation to be like that, and I still find it painful that Michael became a prisoner. Was it this experience that led me to women in prison?

◆   ◆   ◆

It took a long time to get from the moment when I was first struck by the desire to teach meditation to people in prison to the point where I taught my first class. I lived in coastal Massachusetts, and I began by calling the local sheriff. He connected me to the head of prison programs.

"It won't work," he said. "I had a priest offer to do the same thing, and the prisoners wouldn't appreciate it. Don't waste your time." With such encouragement, I let the matter drop for nearly a decade, but a few years ago, my inner voice began murmuring to me again, even more persistently this time.

In the interim, I had gotten certified as a yoga teacher, so I called the only women's prison in Massachusetts and asked if they were interested in a yoga and meditation class. This time the program director, a young woman, sounded enthusiastic, but after a month or so her superiors got back to her with a thumbs-down. I felt frustrated.

The next lead was through a friend whose father was a prison attorney. He gave me a good connection to the department of education within an all-male prison. Once again, I sent in a proposal with an outline. While I waited for the program director to make a decision, I signed up for a tour of this prison. I thought it would help to feel the energy in the place and get a better sense of what it would be like to work inside its walls.

There was a no-skirt rule for visitors. The top floors were made of metal grating, which meant that anyone on a lower floor could look right up a woman's skirt. One high school girl on the tour who hadn't heard of the rule showed up in a mini-skirt. The guard gave her a pair of prison pants to wear under the skirt to prevent a riot.

Two young prisoners spoke to the visitors, who were mostly high school kids, about how they had ended up there. One was an honors student whose girlfriend dumped him for another boy. He got drunk, beat up the boy, broke a window at his ex-girlfriend's house, and drove home to bed. The next morning he was arrested.

The other prisoner was in for dealing drugs. He had been convicted once before. Within twenty-four hours of his release, he landed back in prison for the same offense. His story seemed more typical. He was from a tough, poor neighborhood and had experienced difficulty while finding work. The worst part for him was that none of his so-called friends had ever visited him in jail.

My eyes filled up more than once during the tour. The voice in my head got even stronger. I really felt that yoga and meditation would help these guys. I dropped off a note at the program director's office to let her know that I had been there, hoping to tip the scales. But, no, a new sheriff had just taken office. To make the changeover easier, the programs would stay the same. So, I told my inner voice to shut up.

About six months later at a pool party, a young woman mentioned that she worked in the prison system. I told her my saga, and she put me in touch with Anne Riter, the women's program director at a minimum-security prison for men and women. I spoke with Anne on the phone about my program, and Anne decided we needed to meet in person. Anne studied my proposal and then looked up at me.

"You know, the women really need something like this. A lot of them are overweight because they're so sedentary. Can you take the words 'yoga and meditation' out of your proposal? The powers-that-be frown on these words."

I changed the title to "Fit and Wellness" and called it a course in "stretching" and "guided imagery." With that, Anne Riter was able to push it through.

When we met again, Anne said I would have to make a list of all the things I'd be taking to class, including the titles of the CD music. Everything had to be approved ahead of time. Anne advised me to bring as little as possible. She said that I could tell the prisoners my first name but should keep personal information to a minimum. This was so that no one would try to get in touch with me once they got out. Aside from that, I was going in cold. I felt really glad I'd taken a tour of the men's prison; at least I had some sense of what the surroundings might be like.

Orientation

As I drove up the expressway toward the prison, a misty rain obscured the strip malls and apartment buildings. The wind surging in from the ocean felt raw, bringing down the last bright leaves, making the trees look bedraggled. The traffic was thick with bright yellow school buses and the first-shift rush hour. I was on my way to an orientation at the prison where I was finally going to teach. It had taken me a year to get this course up and running, but at the moment, my biggest worry was how I was dressed.

I wasn't worried about the reactions of the women prisoners who would be my students or even Anne Riter's judgment. I worried about how to dress appropriately for the officers in the lobby. I wanted to look professional but friendly. I wanted to look like part of the team. I knew I couldn't wear a skirt; I had to wear pants comfortable enough to do the stretches in, but they couldn't be too casual. I had ended up in tapered black warm-up pants (not so loose they had baggy knees, not so tight they showed my senior curves), a black turtleneck T-shirt (black is always good) and a long, loose wool sweater in royal blue. Over this outfit, I wore a black trench coat—what I always thought of as my detective coat.

My throat began to tighten, and my mouth felt dry. I wondered if, when I spoke to the officers, trying to make some kind of human contact, my lips would stick to each other. Maybe I wouldn't be able to utter a sound. My throat had always acted up when I began a class. I feared that I'd open my mouth and nothing would come out. I was afraid I'd choke, and then I felt like I was literally choking.

Stuck in traffic, I took some calming breaths. I was going to teach people to relax, so I figured I'd better do it myself.

As I approached the prison, I felt totally lost and couldn't find the exit off the expressway. I saw the building with the Massachusetts flag flying in the breeze, but I couldn't figure out how to get to it. Frantic and wanting to be on time, I followed a sign for a Boston police station. I quickly drove in, parked the car, and dashed up to the front-desk officer for directions. I found myself nervously explaining that I needed to get to the prison for an orientation as a teacher. I certainly didn't want him to think I was going to visit. I followed his directions, and in less than five minutes, I was turning into the main entrance of the prison. I was thrilled to see someone pulling out of a parking place about five hundred feet from the front door.

As I walked up the steps, I noticed many visitors and employees smoking outside—escapees from an indoors smoke-free policy. Prisons were certainly not smoke-free environments. Inside the lobby, my attention was drawn to the large number of prison guards in all sizes and shapes. I wondered about their backgrounds. Were they educated beyond high school? Is a stint of prison work a stepping stone to something else? Are they waiting to get into law school and using this as valuable experience? Do they have families? Loved ones? Are they lonely in their own personal prisons? How does this type of job affect them? I wondered what they did for an outlet when they returned to the "real world."

I sat on a hard, gray bench waiting for Elizabeth Khorn, program director for both the men and women, to appear and begin orientation. The lobby was comfortable, with long attached benches facing the officer's window, but it was not an inviting atmosphere. Television monitors were discreetly placed in each corner of the lobby. I watched the visitors parade in front of me and began to feel their sadness so intensely that I wanted to cry to relieve their pain. I suddenly felt connected with all the crimes committed against mankind over centuries.

I then remembered that my purpose was to work with these inmates in a loving and compassionate way that would help them. *Can I accomplish these goals?* I wondered. *Or will I hide behind rose-colored glasses?* I was about to find out.

As my mind drifted from fantasy to reality, I saw a young girl who sat down next to me. She asked if they had given out forms for the 6:30 PM visitations.

"I'm not sure," I replied. "I heard only a few names called and saw some pink papers floating around."

She appeared calm on the outside, but I felt her repressed nervousness. I asked her if the facility was strictly for women.

"No, the upper two floors are where the women are housed, and the lower floors are for the men." She confided in me that this was her first time at the prison, and she was not sure of all the rules for visitors. She did know, as I later learned, that three times a week, the inmates got to have visits, lasting up to one hour within the limits of the scheduled visiting hours, provided the inmates had not violated any prison rules. She disclosed that most inmates were kept in this prison facility for a maximum of three years.

"My boyfriend told me when we talked on the phone that some guys are here for five years—two consecutive sentences," she confided.

Most were in for drug possession, assault and battery or parole violation, serving one- to three-year sentences. I realized that this might be her boyfriend's first time in prison. I also learned that the age range began at eighteen years old.

She once again became quiet. I understood her silence. I thought of her as a young maiden, because she looked not a day older than seventeen, and she had pure white skin, perfectly curled hair and only a faint hint of make-up. She resembled what I thought Juliet, in *Romeo and Juliet*, might look like. I wondered if her mother knew where she was.

Suddenly, a tall black woman appeared, perhaps in her twenties, in tight jeans with inviting hips. As she walked and swayed back and forth, I wondered who had been invited into her world of social pleasures. Secrets I will never know! I was fascinated with the range of visitors that came into the lobby.

The room began to fill up with a variety of characters. Each represented a unique story. There was a full range of racial and ethnic backgrounds—Hispanic, White, Black and Asian. An old couple, speaking Spanish, fumbled through visitation papers together, appearing confused. When the woman went to the restroom, I saw that her feet were swollen; she could barely walk the short distance. Her face revealed the pain. Her husband sat quietly, holding a lunch bag into which he put a half-eaten sandwich and an emptied can of soda. He burped loudly as if to say, "I'm here!"

A soft-spoken guard began to call names for the 6:30 group to come up front with their forms and be checked for drugs, guns, knives, etc. When the officer finished, he came over to me and asked if I had filled out a pink slip. I politely told him that I was waiting for Elizabeth for orientation. The group was then herded into another room to wait for their loved ones, friends or business associates to emerge from behind the prison bars into the visiting area.

I had been so distracted that I didn't realize that Elizabeth had arrived until I looked up and saw a woman staring at me. She explained that a group had been scheduled for orientation, but they had canceled at the last minute, so the session would not be held. My heart sank.

Here we go again, I thought. *Another roadblock.*

"We'll skip orientation. You can do it another time," Elizabeth said.

All I needed to do was fill out five pages of forms with information about my parents and me, including my mother's maiden name and my residences in the past ten years. I needed to sign a release form giving them permission to do a background check on me to make sure I was an upstanding citizen who had never been in trouble with the law—not even outstanding parking tickets. I knew I was honest, but as I filled out those forms, I wondered if there might be some little thing that I was not remembering. I began to feel my own fears surfacing. Whoa!

When I handed Elizabeth the completed forms, she told me it would take two weeks for the papers to be cleared.

"Call Anne, and she'll give you a starting date," she said. "You can coordinate the particulars with her."

I wished Elizabeth a good day.

What have you gotten yourself into this time? I thought as I left through the front door, still worrying about the clearance. I wanted to give this program of "Fit and Wellness" my best effort. I knew my success would enable others to present similar programs that would help inmates create more positive lives outside of prison and help them realize their hope never to return.

As it turned out, my first week was canceled due to a lockdown, which in my mind (having seen too much TV) meant a riot. Actually, a lockdown occurs not only for disturbances in the unit but also for things like electrical problems. Until it is resolved, no volunteers or visitors come in, and inmates are usually locked in their cells. All programs are canceled until the situation is corrected.

I was entering a new world that used a special language, a world that required patience for adapting to the ever-changing schedules, and a world that required my willingness to accept loss of privacy when entering the facility.

First Class

When I pulled into the parking lot of the prison for my first class, there was no place to park. I'd arrived at a bad time—the changing of shifts. So I competed with the incoming employees until I found a space. I grabbed my purse and the clear plastic baggie that held my CD, glasses and driver's license, and raced up the steps through the cloud of smoke that enveloped the crowd of smokers at the outside entrance.

I had arrived early, wanting to see the classroom and get it ready before the women entered. The lobby swarmed with prison guards—all of them men, most of them big-boned and tall, but some just overweight. I couldn't help thinking that extra weight would make it easier for them to handle an unruly prisoner, even as I wondered how they could do this job and be so out of shape. I also wondered why anyone would want this job. Keeping other people locked up seemed like such a lonely thing to do. Did they do it for the job security? They were all fairly young; maybe some were working their way through school.

I walked up to the front desk, staffed by three officers. I chose the one with the sweet face; I thought he'd be the friendliest.

"Hi," I got out. "I am Veronica Shaffer, and I am doing a volunteer program for the women's unit. Could you call Anne Riter to escort me to my classroom?"

He didn't even look up. He dialed the extension and said, "There is a Veronica Shaffer here." Then, still without bothering to look up, he said, "Go over and sit on the bench until she comes down."

Under my breath I said, "Yes, sir." Then, I sat down to wait.

I had arrived at 2:30 PM so I would have plenty of time to prepare for the women before the 3:00 start time. As I watched the clock, I got more and more nervous, wondering if the class was really going to happen. I couldn't sit still. I asked the officer to call Anne again. He refused. I started pacing back and forth, trying to alleviate my nervousness. At 3:12, Anne finally appeared to inform me she couldn't escort me upstairs herself, because she had another meeting. She also told me that there had been a schedule revision, due to a shift change, so I wasn't able to start class until 3:30. Carolyn, one of the caseworkers from the recovery unit, would get me settled.

Anne took me to the front desk for a visitor's pass. I signed the log book for visitors and volunteers, writing in my car registration number and arrival time. Nervously, I handed the officer my driver's license. Finally, Mr. Not-So-Friendly gave me a locker key for my coat and purse.

"Anne, where is locker number three?" I asked, looking at the key. She pointed, and I hustled. But the key wouldn't open the locker. I tried and I tried. Visitors flowed around me, like I was a rock in the middle of a stream. *What is the matter with this locker? It won't open!*

I looked at the key again and realized that I was in the wrong place. Number three was my visitor pass number; the locker number was fifty-two. I ran to the other side of the lobby and found my locker, which I opened after a brief struggle. With my belongings safely stowed, I breathed again and prayed no one had seen my moment of panic. I hoped this wasn't an omen that someday I would again find myself stuck on the visitor's side. I felt queasy just thinking about anyone from my family being in jail again.

By the time I got back to Anne, she was pissed off about Carolyn not being there yet. Anne's meeting wasn't in the building; she didn't want to be late. Now she was the one who paced and muttered under her breath. "Where is she?" Anne kept repeating.

Carolyn, a small, dark-haired young woman, finally rushed into the lobby, full of apologies. I didn't really listen; I was thinking about getting to the classroom. Anne disappeared and Carolyn took charge. We picked up a CD player in her office, and then got on the elevator. I noticed a video camera in the upper right-hand corner of the elevator car. I wondered if there was a microphone attached. I didn't ask Carolyn, just in case there was one. I felt I should stand up straight and be careful not to fidget (it would look suspicious). I reminded myself to be careful of what I said, because someone might be watching and listening. Then, I realized that I couldn't believe these fearful thoughts were filling my mind. Was this how everyone thought in prison?

A guard was waiting as Carolyn and I came off the elevator.

"This is Bill C., your program officer. He will bring the women to the classroom and take them back to their units or the cafeteria afterward," Carolyn said.

Bill was a balding, muscular man of medium height, with a marine insignia and the word "freedom" tattooed in bold letters on his left arm. He didn't shake my hand or say hello, and he looked like a smile would crack his face. As he unlocked the doors that led into the classroom area, he seemed more interested in the piece of paper Carolyn had given him (the official command to go get the women) than in anything else.

Carolyn and I walked down a short hall to my classroom. The floor was covered with gray linoleum tile. When I took my shoes off, it became a cold slab. The ceiling was speckled sheet rock with huge pieces stained from water damage, and waiting to fall. The walls were bare and painted white except for one that was pea green, as though someone had lost heart before he finished the job. The room was about nine by twelve feet. A large blackboard stood in the center. It was covered with biblical-sounding quotations that admonished the prisoners to "Hear O women the word of the Lord," and "Commit your way to the Lord." This room would have to hold fifteen women doing yoga. I shivered in a draft that flowed from the open ceiling vent; I felt sick again. I needed a miracle to transform this dreary space into a place of healing and renewal.

Carolyn and I moved the blackboard out into the hall. Now I could see the windows. Bars covered two large ones on the outside wall. For one panicky moment, I gave in to the temptation to count the bars on each window. If someone wanted to jump, they would have to starve themselves down to ninety pounds to fit through the bars. On the inside wall was another window, a long narrow one without bars. I looked down through it to a visiting area for prisoners' families and friends, where I saw a large checkerboard and a chessboard, plenty of oversized black leather chairs, and a few weathered benches.

Carolyn brought me back to reality by announcing that the women in blue uniforms would be from the recovery unit—women who were in for crimes related to drug abuse, alcoholism or gambling. Those in brown would be from the general population or GP unit, women who had been convicted for crimes like assault, forgery, robbery, and prostitution.

Carolyn shook my hand and said that she'd be back later to escort me downstairs. She walked out, and suddenly I was on my own. I began the CD of flute music to create a welcoming atmosphere and to calm myself. My ninety-minute class session had already been cut to forty-five minutes. I was trying to figure out what to keep and what to cut when I heard chatter and laughter in the hallway.

Ready or not, here they come, I thought. I stood at the door to welcome them, like the nuns I remembered in Catholic school. It gave me a feeling of being in control.

The sounds of the women coming down the hall, their chirping and "Hey, heys," excited and unnerved me. I wondered how much they felt the impact of being incarcerated. It brought back memories of when I was expecting my third child.

I was twenty-five years old and married to a non-productive alcoholic. He was unemployed, and I could work only a few more months due to my pregnancy. Although working in x-ray during pregnancy was frowned upon, I was allowed to continue because my duties were limited. I was not allowed to work in the operating room or to drag the heavy portable x-ray machine around the hospital, because I would have been exposed directly to radiation. We wore lead aprons, which offered some protection, but working in a room with lead-lined walls was not much safer for a mom and her unborn baby.

In the early sixties, it was unusual for a woman to work full-time, particularly when pregnant. I was definitely in the minority. Women were just starting to come into the work force in great numbers, primarily to finance a house or vacations. What a contrast with today's society, when most women are major breadwinners or work to provide a significant chunk of family income!

I had felt imprisoned and panicky then, with a new baby coming and no secure source of money. We were moving from an apartment to a house, still renting, with no hope of owning our own home. The future looked bleak. The only advantage was that he had no money for alcohol, and his abusive talk ceased. Living under the same roof became bearable for a couple of months until the unemployment checks began to arrive. The verbal abuse started, and fighting once again became our basic way of communicating.

I seethed with emotional turmoil. *How am I going to get out of this hell?* I had wondered then. *How long was my sentence?*

My cell was locked; somehow I had to escape. I cried during the day. Hormones, I told myself, and silently cried myself to sleep at night. *Dear God, what did I do to deserve this sentence?*

Now, as the sounds of the women in the hall returned me to the bare room, I wondered what they thought about their own lives. Did they feel the impact of being in jail or was it easier to deaden the pain than it had been for me in my psychological prison?

The first woman to enter was dressed in brown and must have weighed over 300 pounds. Her uniform didn't fit. The top shirt covered only half of her belly, revealing the bottom hem of a man's t-shirt. Below that, I could see stretch marks and the edge of a scar. The other women filed in past me one by one—some smiling, some looking at me without expression.

The women in brown definitely tended toward obesity. Most of the women were so heavy that one who was probably 200 pounds looked great to me. Despite Anne's warning, I felt unprepared. Most of the women from the recovery unit were fairly thin or only slightly overweight, probably the result of doing drugs. How could I tailor my class to suit such different body types? While I tried to absorb the scene, the women chattered away like a flock of magpies. How could I create order in the chaos? So, I pitched my voice over the noise and asked them to be quiet, clapping my hands to get their attention.

"Sit in a circle on the floor," I said. Then I introduced myself, first name only. "I'm a mother and a grandmother, and I have a medical background." Again, heeding a warning from my program director, *no detailed personal information,* I kept my introduction short. This was difficult for me, because when I taught meditation and yoga outside of prison, I introduced myself in a personal way.

Then I took attendance. When I called one name on the list, no one answered. One of the large black women finally said, "T."

"What?" I asked.

"Termination," she said.

As I went down the list, I learned that "L" meant a woman had been locked up and put in the hole for solitary confinement. A couple of the names were no-shows, and three of the women who had come to class hadn't signed up for it.

So, here I was face to face with "my ladies." There were eight black women, two Native Americans, and three whites. Some of the black women looked Haitian. Some of the hairstyles looked wild, sticking out in all directions, and I wondered if barrettes, curlers and hair dryers were allowed. Did anyone cut their hair? I wouldn't think scissors were permissible. These questions raced through my mind. One woman displayed blonde hair ends and six inches of dark roots. I scanned their faces for some sense of history or feelings, but there was no time to evaluate or guess. I knew nothing about their backgrounds or why they were incarcerated, except for the little that the color of their uniforms told me. The rest was confidential. I couldn't ask, but if they decided to tell me, I could certainly listen.

It had occurred to me that knowing their crimes might make it easier for me to work with them, but I was also just plain curious. I had worked for years in a hospital emergency room, and I loved the thrill of dealing with people in trauma. I got an adrenaline rush—here were the blood and guts. I loved finding out who had caused the trauma and how it was done. It made me feel caught in the action.

The women complained about the cold, damp floor and how cramped they felt. "Hey, you are in prison, not the Boston Health Club," I wanted to say, but they were right.

The floor was cold, and there was barely room to move, even though we sat in a circle to make the most of the space.

As I began talking about the relaxation part of class, a tiny woman named Elberta, with short hair going in all directions, shouted, "If this is meditation, I don't need it, 'cause I meditate every day." She crossed her arms over her skinny chest and lifted her head so she could look down her nose at me.

To defuse the situation, I answered as if her challenge had been a request for information.

"What I do, Elberta," I said, "is a guided imagery, which is a form of meditation. This would be another tool that you could use in your practice."

She looked leery but seemed to have decided to stay.

"Call me Bert," she said. "I don't like the name Elberta, never have. The minister of my parents' church gave me that name. I've got no children or husband, and I'm happy that way."

Some of the women had begun to talk and laugh; I asked for quiet. Then I asked them to go around the circle, introduce themselves, and say a little about why they had chosen this class. In the circle to my left was Cherie, an extremely overweight woman. Her short hair was dark except for fading blonde tips. When she smiled, I could see that her upper teeth were missing on one side.

"I landed in jail because I was working the streets," Cherie began. "I had a good job as a nurse's aide, but I could make more money on the streets. Now that I'm in jail, I realize I can do good work as an aide in a hospital helping people. I won't have to answer to some man about how much money he needs to supply his expensive habits."

Next to Cherie was a Native American woman called Juanita. She was young, probably not even twenty. She sat erectly and spoke her name with pride, "This is my first time in jail, and I have only six weeks left before parole," Juanita said.

Mary sat against the wall. With her head down, she spoke in a soft voice, "I am getting out the end of the month. My kids are fourteen, sixteen, and seventeen, and they are needing me to come home." She was tiny, with shiny hair in two perfect braids. She constantly fidgeted with her shirt. She didn't look old enough to have teenaged children.

Atlanta was next, another large woman. She swayed back and forth in a slow rhythmic motion, all smiles.

"I have been in here before, but I ain't saying how many times." Her brown uniform stretched tautly across her distended abdomen, while her pant legs were rolled up so she wouldn't trip over them.

"I'm here to learn how to exercise and move," she said. "We sit most of the day, and I get lazy and bored. I eat three and four bags of those M&M candies in the canteen every night. Sometimes I switch to a couple of cheese Danish. They sure do make me feel good."

Some of the women only gave their names and then looked to the people next to them, not wanting to talk about themselves.

Halfway around the circle, Twanda spoke. "I have been in and out of jail since I was twelve years old. I get tense and want to beat up people who speak lies about me. Anne Riter told me to do this program to learn how to relax." Twanda was slightly overweight and extremely muscular with a shaved head. She looked very tough.

At the end of the circle sat Delores. She had a large body and a beautiful face with intense, blue eyes. "I am in here for the first time because of drinking and beatin' up my husband. I admit I get mean, the police say violent. My husband or one of the kids called the cops, 'cause they say they can't control me, and here I am for a year."

Once again the women started chirping away; I asked for quiet. Then, I had them remove their shoes so we could get started on the exercises. Twanda and Atlanta joked that they had smelly feet and started the group laughing. Again, I asked for quiet. I couldn't believe how difficult it was to hold their attention.

I told them to close their eyes and connect with their breath, giving them an opportunity to feel their connection to their own breathing body. I thought that some of the difficulty they had in relaxing and being quiet was because they were so disconnected from experiencing their own bodies. I asked the women to open their eyes slowly for the first exercise, a simple warm-up.

"Put your hands on your hips," I said. "Stay seated, slow-ly move your upper body clockwise and then slow-ly repeat in a counterclockwise direction." Although I thought this would be fairly easy, I heard some moaning and grunting as they began to move.

Trying to inspire them, I said, "This is a great stretch to do first thing in the morning. It releases tension in the lower back and opens the hips and pelvis."

Atlanta seemed to catch the spirit. She drew the attention of the class with her pelvic moves and grooves.

"I'm ready for you, I'm ready for you. Come and get me," she sang under her breath. "Pretend you're working the streets," she said to the group. That brought snickers.

"All right, quiet," I said. "We don't have much time. Every minute counts."

As I remember this, I can't help but laugh. At the time, though, I felt irritated with their inability to stay focused.

I had them do a few more stretches on the floor, mostly forward and backward bends, to release tension in the spinal column. I paid close attention to them, especially the larger ones, to see how far they were able to extend. I wanted them to push themselves to their individual edges, but not to hurt themselves.

"Don't force yourself to the point of the posture being painful," I said. "If you keep practicing daily, then each time you will go a little deeper into the pose."

When it was time for them to stand up, some of the heavier women had trouble, and the others gave them assistance. Again, I heard a chorus of loud groans. Atlanta, Cherie, Twanda, and Juanita complained most vocally. They sounded as though they were being tortured.

I wanted them to experience at least one posture for focus and concentration, so I had them do the tree pose, which also helps balance.

"Stand with all your weight on your right leg, and then put your left foot on your right ankle," I instructed them.

With their hands together as in prayer, I had them move the left foot slowly up the right leg, to connect with the right knee. Atlanta and Cherie, the heavy ones, wobbled. I suggested they take one hand and place it on the wall to help balance. I was pleased to see that half the women could get their left foot up to their right knee on the first try. What I hadn't anticipated was that some of them didn't know their right from their left. I circulated through the class, helping them, adjusting their legs or hands as unobtrusively as I could.

With only ten minutes left, I had them lie down on the floor, flat on their backs.

"Bend your knees to your chest, I instructed, Gently rock from side to side, giving your lower back and internal organs a wonderful massage."

Twanda and Cherie were reluctant to put their heads on the floor. "That floor's dirty," Twanda said. "I ain't putting my head there." When they saw me lie down they decided to join the rest of us.

I asked the women to be aware of their aches and pains during the week so I could give them different postures to do at our next class. A lot of them immediately complained about their backs hurting. They had only thin mattresses to sleep on, and it took them awhile to get moving in the morning.

"This is a great position to do on the floor of your cell," I said. I really had a hard time using that word. Maybe I should have said room. I encouraged them by saying that if they did these exercises during the week, they would begin to feel much better.

Then it was time for the guided imagery.

"Close your eyes ... breathe slowly ... give your body permission to relax. I'd like you to go to a place of peace and quiet where you won't be disturbed," I instructed. "Allow that feeling of peace and tranquility to totally fill your body."

They were just beginning to relax when I noticed Carolyn motioning to me through the glassed-in part of the door. It was their dinnertime, and my first class was over.

I wondered how tranquil they could have gotten in five short minutes. I guided them back to an awakening state and thanked them for joining the class. There hadn't been time to allow the women total relaxation or to share their thoughts about the meditation. I felt like the class had been a disaster.

Then Atlanta thanked me on her way out. "You're coming again, right?" she asked.

Next, Atlanta, Juanita, Sylvie and Cherie all said that they felt good and they'd see me next week. Then they hurried across the hall to the cafeteria.

I gathered up the CD player, attendance sheet and baggie and headed for the elevator with Carolyn, anxious to get outside and breathe. In the hall, I smelled an assortment of aromas, all of them appalling: boiled cabbage, old fish, and fried Spam. As we passed the cafeteria, I wondered what was for dinner. If I had the choice of eating whatever smelled like that or candy, I knew which one I would choose.

I said good-bye to Carolyn in the lobby. After my trial by fire, I could hardly wait to get home. I couldn't believe I had just finished my first class in prison. I wondered what kind of impression I made on the women and how many of them would return the following week.

The Tibetan Bells

After the excitement of leading my first class, it was a letdown when class was canceled for the next two weeks due to major repairs of an elevator. Each of those weeks, I called the afternoon of class and felt disappointed when I heard that no visitors, teachers or volunteers were permitted inside the facility. This was one example of a lock-down. All the inmates had to stay in their cells except for meals and bathroom visits.

I felt frustrated, thinking about what I considered the disaster of the first class. I wondered how I could rectify things. Their chattiness worried me most; holding their attention and keeping them quiet were the challenges. I suddenly remembered that I had a pair of Ting-sha Cymbals I used for my own meditation group. They made such a strong vibrating sound that anyone would immediately stop talking and pay attention. *Perfect*, I thought. I called Anne and explained my need. I held my breath.

"Yes, but let's call them bells," she said.

"I'll call them anything you want as long as I can use them in the classroom," I said. I knew the next class would be better.

When the lockdown ended, I headed to the prison on a beautiful, late-fall day. The leaves were falling, and soon the trees would be bare. I felt winter approaching. The waves of Boston Harbor looked calm-ing, and even the expressway traffic wasn't congested. All good signs for me.

As I walked into the lobby, I saw only three officers—two at the front desk and one at the detector. I wondered where all the visitors were; they had started to filter in by 2:30 the last time. The lobby had felt like Grand Central Station, with family and friends anxiously waiting to visit their loved ones. I wondered if a partial lockdown was still in place.

I went up to the officer in charge and gave him a welcoming smile. "It's me again. Could you page Anne Riter?" I asked lightly.

This time he rewarded me with a smile instead of a scowl. *Things are improving,* I thought. Anne impressed me by appearing within five minutes of the page. I dealt with the locker routine without hassle and showed Anne my CD, which she had forgotten to write up.

"There should be no problem," she said coolly.

I shook my Tibetan bells for her, and they rang melodiously. Again, she had forgotten to write these up for approval to bring to class. I tried to hide my frustration as she suggested we go through the detector with them to see what would happen. I felt elated when I breezed through without a problem. The sounds of the bells, I hoped, would save my voice and bring the women to attention more quickly.

Bill C., the program officer, looked angry as he greeted us. He told Anne that his captain had reprimanded him for not being with us at the last class, when, in fact, he *had* been with us. Even though Anne promised to explain the whole scenario to his captain and told him not to worry, Bill continued to scowl. When he finally calmed down, it struck me that maybe the inmates weren't the only ones who needed my class!

Bill C. had Anne's CD player in hand as he led me to the class-room. I shook his hand as he was leaving, reintroducing myself, and again asked for his name.

"Bill C.," he replied.

I sure felt relieved to see a smile. I turned on the relaxing CD music and waited anxiously for the women to arrive. This time I was prepared; I wouldn't have to sound like one of my grade-school nuns to keep order.

The ladies from the recovery unit began arriving much earlier than they had for the first class, so I decided an hour's session was possible.

These women were much thinner than the GP ladies, and again, I wondered if drugs and alcohol had lessened their appetites. They hurriedly sat on the floor, to make sure no one took their preferred spaces.

"Can you take your shoes off?" I suggested. "You'll feel more comfortable doing these exercises."

Fantasia removed her shoes and laughed at the big hole in one of her socks. She wiggled her toe to make the hole larger. This caught the eyes of Jesse and Delores, who began to snicker, making some of the other women reluctant to take off their own sneakers.

"I have smelly feet," Bette said timidly.

Some of the other women chimed in, "I don't want to stink up the room."

I took off my own shoes and assured them it wouldn't bother me. They all wore white socks, and I noticed some were whiter and in better shape than others. I wondered if they were responsible for their own laundry.

The women from the general population unit arrived ten minutes later, having been transported from another floor. They strolled in, Atlanta leading, followed by Cherie and Twanda, and I was surprised to see all three smiling broadly at me. I felt welcomed into their group.

Atlanta eased into the center of the circle, sat right under the window, took her shoes off and adjusted her large brown body to sit comfortably. Her eyes followed my every move. I wondered what images she had in her head about me. Cherie moved next to the CD player, in the same position as the previous week, and sat against the wall for support. She had difficulty crossing her legs, so she extended them out straight. Twanda sat in the far corner to my left and kept her head down, waiting for the other women to enter. She began to do pelvic circles to loosen her lower body.

More ladies rushed in and looked for empty spaces, while others squeezed in between some apparently old friends from the recovery unit. I heard a few comments about when they were getting paroled, how much time they had left, and other light talk about their units. I was amused by Jesse's comments to Twanda: "How's the lockdowns at your place? We's been having a lot lately. We spend more time in than out of our cells. It ain't fair."

The conversation was very different from ones I would have with my friends. We talk about work, clients, social events, and life's activities we enjoy in freedom.

While taking the roll call, Bette informed me that two of the women, Nanci and Julia, had been "terminated." I hesitated to ask what this might mean in prison terms, thinking possibly their lives were ended, when Atlanta spoke up.

"They's on the outside lookin' in," she said.

Everyone else was back. I felt especially surprised to see that the large women had returned. No matter how few exercises they did, I thought it was important to give them an opportunity to connect to their physical bodies. I welcomed them, and like a schoolteacher, I asked if anyone remembered my name.

The room echoed as they responded, "No."

I felt discouraged. If they didn't remember my name, it seemed unlikely they would remember any of the exercises we had performed. I asked if anyone had done stretches during the past week. Surprisingly, three of the women from the recovery unit nodded. Jesse, Alice and Bette then demonstrated the stretches with pride, and I felt encouraged. They stood up and bent forward and backward, moving in unison and with great flexibility. I moved my eyes slowly to catch the expressions from the other women as they intently watched those three do their thing.

"How did you feel after the last class?" I asked.

Their faces lit up and some said, "Alive." I saw great potential for change in these women's approaches to life and to their bodies.

I rang my bells firmly to draw their attention. I explained that ringing the bells twice meant dismissal of anyone who made noise or acted out in an inappropriate manner. When I rang the bells once I wanted silence. Well-accustomed to a rule-laden structure, they nodded, and so we began relaxing by closing our eyes. I directed them to take a few deep breaths in and exhale slowly, releasing tension and stress from their bodies. Gently, the women opened their eyes and stood as I began the stretching. I planned to repeat some exercises from the first week but also to incorporate new postures to stimulate them. They were paying attention to my instructions even though some had difficulty standing without holding onto the wall for support. I encouraged them to use the wall or a chair back in their unit until they felt comfortable without them.

An officer who was new to me abruptly entered the room.

"Rodriguez and Hollis, come with me!" he shouted.

Two women from the GP unit left quickly, and I wondered what that was all about. It was hard not to get rattled in such a class environment, but I tried to continue as if nothing had happened. We worked through simple, moderate, and a few challenging exercises, learning some new postures. I didn't want to let them get bored; I knew they needed motivation.

Rodriguez and Hollis returned and whispered something to the women next to them. I couldn't hear, but I sensed they weren't happy about being called away from class.

I asked the ladies to partner up, just as we had the first week. This time, I demonstrated with Juanita bent forward in a rag-doll position, while Jessie placed one hand on the nape of her neck and the other hand on the bottom of her spine, gently pressing and supporting Juanita to extend further down, lengthening her spinal column. I then had them tap up and down their partners' backs; it was a light massage, and they loved it. This was a wonderful way to stimulate the tissues, muscles, and the spinal column.

Partner work seemed to be a big hit, so I made a mental note to do at least one such exercise each week. It must give them a feeling of support, as touching was otherwise off-limits in prison. I wanted more insight, so I decided to check this out with my psychotherapist later.

I asked the women to lie down on the floor, but again they resisted, protesting that the floor was dirty. Yielding, I added exercises they could perform on their knees instead. I had them place their palms flat on the floor under their shoulders, with their knees directly under their hips, to make a flat back, called *table position*. I then had them wiggle their hips from left to right, like windshield wipers. This was great for loosening their hips and pelvises. The floor was hard and some complained that their knees hurt. Atlanta just sat on the floor and watched the others. Cherie tried but got up and stood against the wall. I sensed the linoleum was placed over cement. I realized, for the women that postures done on their knees, without mats, would be impossible.

Relaxation time was their favorite part of the class. I asked them to become comfortable, either lying or sitting on the floor.

"Close your eyes. Give yourself permission to relax. Breathe. Be aware of your breath, and let go of any stress or tension in your body. I would like you to visualize a place where you feel safe, one where you feel peaceful and calm." I waited a few seconds before I continued. "Give yourself permission to be in that peaceful place, being aware of your surroundings, the scents and colors." I gave them a few minutes to adjust to this guided imagery. "Allow your heart to open and receive the love and support that is around you. Bring a flower to your heart. See that flower as a bud. Allow it to bloom and blossom, remembering the color and appearance of the flower." I let them absorb that image. "Remember this flower, and keep it as a symbol of love and support. Watch it grow through the week by periodically closing your eyes and bringing your flower back into your mind's eye."

It is a simple but effective way to practice stillness and connect with love. I asked if anyone wanted to share with the group about her experience, and several raised their hands.

"I was swimming and the water felt warm," Twanda said. "I didn't want to get out."

Alice said that she was in a desert, alone and sad, while Jesse excitedly explained a long scenario about all the flowers that came to her. I listened intently to their visualizations.

Suddenly, I heard a tap on the window. Bill C. was announcing dinnertime. I had the ladies stand quickly and asked that we all hold hands. I thanked them for a great class. I didn't want them to feel abruptly disconnected. I encouraged them to practice some of the exercises during the week and to take quiet time for themselves.

"Listen to your body," I urged.

I wished them a good week as they left. Christmas was in two weeks, and I wondered about the holidays and how they would be spent in prison.

"You better keep coming back on Thursdays," several said.

I assured them that I would.

As I waited for the elevator, I saw Sue and Cherie marching into the cafeteria, and I put my hand up to gesture a "high five." They didn't respond, and I felt disappointed. Later, it dawned on me that I had been instructed not to mingle with the women outside of my class. I feared that I would be reprimanded for that action. There were so many new rules to absorb.

"Go slowly," I thought. "Stop and think before acting."

Bill C. brought Frank, yet another new face, to escort me out of the building. I learned that he was a social worker as we rode down in the elevator. He had been transferred here when another correctional facility closed. Reluctantly, he had taken this new position. As I walked out of the lobby, I looked up at the deep blue sky and saw a plane flying overhead. I suddenly wished I were up there, too.

"Thank God, I'm only here once a week," I thought.

Being the Stranger

I was sitting on the bench waiting for Anne Riter to escort me upstairs for my class. The wait-and-show was becoming part of the system, and I wasn't sure I liked it. Patience wasn't one of my virtues. I noticed Patrick, my bald-headed, bearded friend, who was wearing his usual turn-me-off, turn-me-on happy face—depending on what, I didn't have a clue. I was bored with staring at a desolate lobby, and I was tired of watching the hands of the clock move slowly. I rummaged through my pocket and found a red and blue ballpoint pen. I opened my date book to a blank page. I decided I was going to imagine how Patrick felt about himself and people in general.

> *I, Patrick Mallory, have been working this desk job here at the jail for the past fifteen years. At times, I feel I could choke all the women in this prison, both employees and inmates, for their lack of intelligence, and punch the lights out of every male who steps forward to visit his family, friend or business associate.*
>
> *I have lost respect for anyone or anything that enters this facility, be it prisoner or visitor. I fall into the category of the song, "Hard-Hearted Hannah," or more appropriately, "Hard-Hearted Harry."*
>
> *I am the ultimate authority as to whether any outside visitor goes beyond this line. I am not ashamed to admit there is a certain rush that goes through me when I have the opportunity to use my power.*
>
> *Today is Thursday—the busiest day of the week. It is the first of the month, which means welfare and social security checks are in the hands of half of our visitor population. For a lot, it means a new supply of drugs and alcohol to get them through most of the month. I wonder how many of the visitors will arrive with a toot on. It's disgusting how many show up loud and disorderly. I get the privilege of*

saying, "*Out!*" *Sometimes we even have a scuffle, but since I've put on forty pounds in the past three months, it isn't as easy to wrestle with a bad apple. I really need to start going to the gym and working with a diet center, but since my wife has been in the hospital with MS, I just don't have the enthusiasm for keeping in shape. Running back and forth to the hospital, keeping up the household chores and commuting thirty miles each way to work doesn't give me much time to get into a healthy physical regime.*

Well, well, well. Look who's coming through the doors early today! I notice the blonde bitch sauntering across the lobby. This woman of distinction, as she would like me to think of her, comes in every Thursday to volunteer her services to the females up on the eleventh floor for a program called Fit and Wellness—some kind of stretching and meditation, but I hear whispers it's really yoga. If I could prove that she is doing yoga, she would be out on her ass ASAP. I heard yoga is some kind of postures where you contort your body and chant until you leave your body. This type of practice is most definitely dangerous to our prisoners. In no way can I see the benefits of such nonsense. Most of them are on the edge of flipping out anyway, and this would finish the job.

Could you imagine the newspapers getting wind of these happenings? The headlines reading, "Boston prisoners claim yoga program allows them to leave their bodies and indulge in astral travel."

Politically speaking, our dear elected sheriff would be out of a job. We need to keep the taxpayers abreast of the good works we are performing for our prisoners so they know where their money is being used which is the only chant we hear.

Here she is at the desk, looking for Charlie to take care of her, as always. He gives her special treatment, talking and smiling at her as he speaks. I call it flirting.

This is the moment I have been waiting for. "Hi," she greets me in that meditative voice that chills my spine as if someone ran a fingernail across the blackboard.

"How are you today?" she continues, as if I am supposed to make small talk.

Not me. I have a job to do. No time for her chatter.

"Do you have your driver's license?" I ask her in my power tone, and then realize she is already handing it to me. I take the license and give her a visitor's pass, along with a key for a locker for her coat and pocketbook. I deliberately give her a key for the visitors' lockers

instead of a key for the lawyers' lockers that Charlie always gives her—putting her in an elevated status on the other side of the room. Segregation you could call it. Let her feel what it is like to be one of the visitors. I put the stamper out to imprint our emblem on her hand, which is invisible but can be detected under ultraviolet light when going through the scanner. I stamp a little harder than usual, hoping she'll wince.

Blondie always brings with her a CD—music I never recognize—some kind of bells, a pencil and glasses in a clear plastic bag. All her items have to be pre-approved before she can take them upstairs for her program. I look at the book for the written authorization, and I don't see the bells written in for approval. So I say in my power voice, "You need to leave the bells here. They are not pre-approved."

"I always have approval for the bells," she says in an anxious voice. "There must be some mistake. You need to call Anne Riter at extension 22, and she will talk with you," Blondie tells me.

"They are not in the book, so leave them here. You talk to her when you go upstairs!"

Blondie says a little louder but with a controlled voice, "I really need these bells for my program."

I am beginning to lose my cool. "I told you the rules, so you have a choice. Go up to do the program or leave; it's that simple." I watch her as she hesitates, turns to go upstairs, stops and comes back.

Almost in a pleading voice she says, "Please call Anne for me, and she will straighten this out."

I imitate her Blondie voice. "Anne has gone for the day. Make up your mind, and do it quickly. I have a line of people waiting to be checked in."

"You bastard," I hear her say under her breath, and that's all I need to hear.

"Ms. Shaffer, I heard your words of endearment. You need to remove yourself from the premises now. If you don't, I will call for backup to escort you out. Profanities are not tolerated here in our facility."

Her face is a glow of red as she turns and proceeds to leave the building. I am overcome with joy, having had this moment to take that bitch down. This is better than an orgasm. I'll do a written report to cover myself. The next time Blondie comes in here, she'll know to bow her head in humility. I may even ask that she verbally apologize for her profanity or else refuse her entry again. What a great day this turned out to be!

I was still busy writing when I heard someone ask, "Is that a letter you're writing?"

I glanced up, and there was Anne, staring at me, ready to go upstairs. I jumped up and followed her toward the elevator, too nervous to ask if she had been waiting long. Fortunately, my fantasy about Patrick Mallory was only a fantasy.

Christmas and the Full Moon

I felt apprehensive driving to prison two days after Christmas. There would be a full moon that night. When I worked in the hospital emergency room, I had noticed that we were busier and treated more traumas during the holiday season, and that patients, as well as associates, seemed more emotional during a full-moon cycle. Crying and outbursts of anger were often rampant.

As I turned into the parking lot, a giant yellow bulldozer confronted me, and there was no one directing traffic. I knew only one route into the prison. Unfamiliar with the rest of the area and feeling panicky that I would be late for class, I backed out onto a busy street to find an alternate way.

"Typical Massachusetts construction," I thought. I asked a man walking in my direction for help in finding the prison.

He graciously advised me, started to walk away from my car then abruptly turned back and asked, "Are you going to visit someone in there?"

"No, I am teaching a class to help inmates get out of there," I replied.

He nodded and continued on his way, obviously feeling better about me. I wondered what he would have said if I had told him a horrific tale, like I was visiting a serial killer who had once been my lover. I smiled to myself and continued driving.

Anne had called during the week to say that a new social worker, Marie, would escort me to class. Would I have to page and re-page her as with the others? The new starting time for class, thirty minutes later than before, made parking easier to find on the street. The brisk walk, two blocks to the prison, was a good way to relax. When I entered the lobby, I felt even more comfortable than I had the previous week. The motions were all familiar now: going up to the desk to receive my key for the locker, handing over my driver's license to the officer, and receiving my visitor's pass. The officers now recognized me and smiled. John Jacobs, as his badge identified him, became more helpful each week. As he searched his files for Marie's page number, I heard, "Veronica Shaffer?"

I looked up to see a pretty, petite woman with huge green eyes and silver hair, long and braided, standing in front of me.

"I'm here to escort you upstairs to your classroom. I'm Marie," she said in a welcoming tone.

Bill C., who waited in the hallway to call the units to bring the women up for class, was much friendlier and chatted about where he lived and how a long commute affected his workday. Leaving his house at 1:00 PM to be on duty in full dress uniform by 2:25, then departing from the prison at midnight and arriving home at 1:00 AM made for a long day. I understood why he already felt stressed when he came on duty.

The ladies from the recovery unit arrived first again, and settled in their favorite places in the room. As I started to take attendance, I noticed Alice was absent. She was one who really seemed to take an interest in everything I taught.

"Where's Alice?" I asked.

"She's taking a shower and didn't feel like coming," Atlanta answered.

I remembered that in the previous week's guided imagery, Alice had traveled to a desert where she saw a beautiful flower growing. I didn't understand the significance, so I had spoken with my therapist who thought that this imagery suggested someone who had not experienced nurturing. Her desert flower grew where there was obviously little water. I wondered if Alice had begun to feel the pain of the holidays or the lack of loved ones nearby for support. Her family lived out of state.

"My so-called friends don't come to visit. I ain't seen no one since I've been in this hole," she had said in the previous class.

The work we were doing brought up a lot of feelings. It could be difficult for someone not used to experiencing her emotions, especially when there was no outside support system. I hoped I would see her the next week but reminded myself not to have unreal expectations. The concept of doing my program and letting the results unfold in whatever ways they might was difficult for me. I felt grateful that I regularly worked with a therapist who provided the opportunity to process my own feelings.

"How was Christmas?" I asked the ladies. "What did you do?"

"No tree and no gifts," Cherie and Atlanta said in a sad tone. "We were going to sing Christmas carols, but some women were fighting, so that privilege was taken away."

"It sucked!" Twanda said bluntly.

I wanted to remind them that in prison you relinquish the right to live outside in a free society that delights in celebrating holidays. Instead, I listened for a while, and then said, "Unfortunately, in this system, when a few act up, all are punished. Outside, you could walk away from those troublemakers and not get involved."

I wondered if they got the message, and then changed the subject.

"Who remembers my name?" I asked, hoping for a positive response this time.

"Ronnie," nearly everyone shouted. Finally, they were connecting with me.

"Who did any of the exercises?"

I got a few positive responses. Cherie piped up that she had been getting stressed out when working with her social worker and remembered to do some shoulder rolls. It worked for her, and she felt surprised.

Yeah! I cheered silently.

Bert sat outside the circle again, still apparently feeling that the program did not work for her. She had continued mumbling that she did her own meditation already and could not see how the class would help her. She seemed locked into a negative attitude. Some women from the addiction unit thought she was not ready to give up her alcohol addiction. She constantly challenged the teacher in the twelve-step program, they told me, when I tried to encourage her to join us.

"It's about giving up control; letting go, letting God take control," Juanita said to Bert.

I decided to change tactics and told Bert that if she wanted to leave, then she should leave, and maybe try it again in a couple of months. Seemingly surprised at my response, she marched out with what looked like an air of indignation.

"When you think you have all the answers, that's when you don't have any," I said to the group. This class provided an opportunity for the women to find new avenues of support, but some would turn away.

"What exercises could I do for my tummy?" Leona asked. "I had a C-section eight weeks ago. I know diet is a big part of my problem," she admitted sheepishly.

I demonstrated the stomach-strengthening twist. If she practiced regularly, I assured her, weak abdominal muscles would grow noticeably stronger in a shorter time. Next week, I would talk to them about what they ate in the cafeteria and the canteen.

Pleased with how well the class had gone, I left feeling hopeful that things were finally falling into place.

◆   ◆   ◆

As I approached the front desk for my fourth class, John Jacobs was nowhere in sight. I felt uncomfortable as I asked an officer I hardly knew to page Anne Riter.

"There's no answer," he said abruptly.

I wondered if there would be yet another new person to greet me. I was annoyed by these changes week after week.

"Listen," he said sharply. "You've been going to the lockers reserved for attorneys and politicians." He pointed to the row of visitors' lockers. "Start going over there."

I understood from his tone that he was exercising his power. It was just as I had imagined it from Officer Mallory. I felt so irate, I couldn't look at him. I made a mental note to check his badge for a name just as Anne appeared, and I jumped at the chance to greet her. It felt good to be away from the vibes of this would-be Napoleon.

Each week, I introduced music that relaxed the ladies and improved their focus. That day, I planned to incorporate more breathing techniques, because mind and breath are interrelated. Calming the breath helps to quiet the mind.

Anne had a meeting to attend, so she put me on the elevator, passing her employee badge over the screen, and pressed eleven. My program officer would meet me at the elevator. As the doors opened, a handsome black man was there, waiting for me. He extended his huge hand as an introduction, "I'm James Wilson."

He had already called both units, and I heard the familiar sounds of the women coming down the hall.

They hurriedly pushed into the room and seated themselves in their usual places. I looked around. Bert, the woman I had asked to leave, had not returned. I was grateful that there wouldn't be a confrontation. Alice, who hadn't shown up the previous week, was also absent again. I wondered why she had decided not to return, but I wouldn't be privileged to know.

I saw James stop a new face outside the room.

"Your name is not on this list. Go back to your unit," he said. His tone was unpleasant.

She turned, head down, and slowly walked toward her unit. James looked at me and shook his head in disgust. I wondered if he would reprimand her later or complain to one of the officers in the unit.

"Two weeks left, and you'll receive a certificate of completion for this Fit and Wellness program," I reminded the women. "Don't forget to write your paper about how the program helped you."

They nodded, and Atlanta asked, "How many pages?"

"A few sentences, three or four, but no more than a page," I reminded them.

We talked about nutrition and the kind of food they ate in prison. The cafeteria did not have a salad bar and rarely offered second helpings. The meals were high in carbohydrates. They ate mostly late at night in the canteen—candy bars, chips, and Danishes. I would have been lost without a salad bar and choice of foods in my daily life. I wondered what they did when a meal was served they didn't like; they probably waited for the evening canteen. Families were not allowed to bring food to prisoners.

I decided this would be a good time to use the word "choice" in my conversation.

"You have an advantage here, because there are fewer food choices," I said. "Outside, we are tempted too often by a choice of foods that are not healthy."

I reminded them that choices are everywhere, not only in food, but in all aspects of life. I suggested that they stop and think about choosing unwisely and ending up back in prison again. Again, I hoped they got the message, and then moved the topic back squarely on class.

During relaxation time, I noticed that one of the ladies, Dee, tried to poke Mary to annoy her. Mary didn't know I'd seen Dee do this several times. Mary looked frustrated.

"Stop, or leave the class," I said to Dee.

Dee had a smug look on her face. As she listened, she looked as though she wanted to say something but decided that silence was best for the moment. If she acted out again the following week, I would report her to Anne. She had already missed one class, and I didn't like inappropriate behavior.

◆   ◆   ◆

During the week, Anne called me.

"You can use parking lot A. I got a special sticker for you," she said. "Just sign in at the front desk with your license number, color, and make of your car."

I thanked her and wondered how this fortune had come about but knew that there were times to keep quiet and accept the good that may come.

Peter Becomes an Ally

I dreaded seeing the Napoleon who had chastised me about my locker and hoped Marie would be waiting for me in the lobby. The thought of him confronting me made me nauseated.

When I arrived for my next class, I was surprised to see many more people than usual lined up in the lobby for visitation. I scanned the room, thinking that most of them probably didn't work. A large number of children had come with a parent to visit a loved one, probably another parent. I spotted a newborn baby. Her mother was breastfeeding her while grasping the hand of another child, who tried desperately to move away. I saw men in three-piece suits and a perfectly manicured woman in a fur coat. My eyes fell back on the little ones. I felt sad that these young children had to be exposed to prison life.

"What is happening?" I asked Napoleon. "This place looks like the emergency room at Johns Hopkins Hospital, where I used to work," I finished by way of explanation and took the moment to glance at Napoleon's chest.

His badge said "Peter Hanley." He explained that it was always busy like this after a lockdown was cleared. There had been a small riot in one of the men's units. A couple of officers had some bruises and one had a back injury. Inmate privileges had been taken away for a week, which also meant that visitors were not permitted. In two of the men's units, where these incidents had happened, privileges had been revoked for three weeks.

Peter then confessed that his ten years of working in the prison system had almost blown his mind. He had experienced a nervous breakdown and spent six months on sick leave.

"I meditate every day," he said.

I realized then that he had read my profile, which explained the type of program I taught.

"You should be in my class," I said, relieved that his attitude had changed toward me.

"I work out daily in a gym close to my home," he said. "It's my salvation."

"Try yoga for deeper relaxation," I suggested.

He nodded. "I may do that," he added.

I reflected again that the type of program I taught would be perfect for the officers, even if it were offered only monthly. Most worked out in a physical way, but connecting their bodies to their emotional lives was equally important to their overall health.

As I sat waiting for Marie, I saw a small Jewish man who I'd noticed on a number of previous visits. He frequently wore a yarmulke and always looked sad. Hunched over, he constantly paced the floor, anxiously awaiting his time with a loved one. He nodded to several of the visitors as they arrived. He probably had developed a kinship with some of them.

An older black woman in her late seventies entered the lobby, wearing a skintight denim skirt with a slit up the back from her ankles to just beneath her buttocks. The skirt was so tight, she could barely walk. My attention was drawn to the backs of her legs as she strutted by. I saw one knee-high stocking on one leg and a thicker one on the other, the type that is used as support for varicose veins. She wore red spikes, and I wondered how she was able to get in and out of a car. Walking along the cement pavements certainly must have posed a problem for her.

Suddenly, nine male prisoners walked into the lobby with an officer. The prisoners wore yellow sweatshirts with the prison name embroidered on the front. They were members of the outside work crew who cleaned the highway debris, trimmed trees, and planted greenery. Good behavior had earned them this reward.

In the classroom, the ladies seemed to be in a cheerful mood overall, and I felt happy to see how they had progressed in their exercises. They continued to complain about their backs and necks hurting, and they asked if they could do some partner forward bends, which had been such a hit in previous weeks.

"This is way better than my man, Elwood, beating on my back," shouted Dee.

No one touched that remark.

Once again, I stressed the importance of continuing to do these exercises in their rooms. I was still struggling saying "cells," and I wasn't sure what the inmates called them. Rooms seemed a safe word for now.

As Mary was leaving class, she stopped and said, "You look like someone I saw working in Victoria's Secret."

I jokingly replied that my husband would find that statement amusing, picturing me in those sexy outfits that I don't wear.

◆   ◆   ◆

Another week canceled because of a lockdown.

I was beginning to wonder if this class would ever complete its six sessions.

Class resumed the following week, and some of the women started talking about ancestry. The conversation began when I was taking roll call and I commented on Jeorgina's name.

"It sounds Native American," I said.

Jeorgina spoke proudly of being from the Sioux lineage, and another woman, Shanee, said she was Iroquois. Choni chimed in that her mother was Cherokee. They had all studied their ethnic backgrounds through the books in the prison library.

As the women left class, I reminded them, again, to bring their papers the following week. I explained the importance of their testimonials about the program so I could have validation when asked how the inmates responded to this type of exercise program.

"Could we sign up for the next session?" several of the ladies asked.

I told them I would speak with Anne and let them know.

I shared with Anne that I felt anxious about some of the group repeating the course. I worried that if they found it "old hat," they could be more of a detriment than an example. Anne decided that the heavy women needed to continue.

"There is a new group of twelve signed up to do the program," she said.

Her words were encouraging. I felt I was there to stay.

◆   ◆   ◆

We made it to the sixth session!

Marie and I went through the routine checking in and stopped by Anne's office to get the certificates. Anne and I signed them, and she looked up after the last one to say, "This is a great program. Keep up the good work."

I was thrilled. I had made it. After the long struggle of trying to get into a correctional facility, I had proven myself to the staff and inmates.

I waited in the classroom, excited to hand the ladies their certificates and to read their papers. Atlanta sauntered in first and handed me her paper. Cherie walked past me. Dee and Mary hurried to their places in the circle, and I saw no papers. Choni handed me hers, and the rest of the women came in and joined their friends on the floor without passing in their assignments. They were their usual chatty selves, and I rang the bells for attention.

"Pass in your papers," I said.

"I forgot to do it," several chorused.

Others said, "I didn't have time."

I wondered what could have kept them so busy. Disappointed, I told them there would be a seventh session. If they did their assignment, there would be graduation. I told Twanda and Bette they had to make up two classes before they received their certificates. To my surprise, some of the women said, "That's only fair."

I expressed my disappointment that they weren't prepared, and Twanda and Mary hung their heads, embarrassed. They both did their exercises without groaning and paid close attention to my instructions. Best of all, there was no chirping.

After the meditation, Bette shared with us that she had been to court that morning and would be released at five o'clock. She was having a hard time containing herself and her excitement rushed through the others. I asked Bette to sit in the center and for the ladies to send her off with positive thoughts for her new life. They gave some wonderful affirmations:

"Follow your dreams."

"Don't screw up and put yourself back in here."

"We will miss your laugh and smile."

"Keep God on your side."

"Continue to walk in the path of light, and always know that there is support no matter how hard life becomes," I added.

Tears flowed down Bette's cheeks as she listened to the group.

I felt inquisitive that day and asked them if they wanted to share how much time they had left and what their goals were upon parole.

Jeorgina spoke first.

"I've been here for one year, and if I can keep my hands to myself, I'll pick up time for good behavior. Amen," she added.

The ladies clapped and said, "You'll make it!"

Shanee had only thirty days left but opted to stay another thirty instead of an early release with parole. She was thinking about moving to a New York reservation with her Iroquois family and counseling young adults on the dangers of drugs and alcohol.

Atlanta voiced her determination to have an exercise room in her basement but felt she needed to spend time in Quincy House, a half-way residence program where the women were counseled in preparation for re-entering society. She didn't feel secure enough to be around family and friends.

Frances said she preferred not to answer about time left to serve but shared that her goal was to have a better relationship with her children. She always wanted to talk; I felt surprised that she seemed so reserved about the length of her prison term.

Most of the women had between three to six months left to serve and expressed their anxieties about getting home to their children.

Class ended on a positive note, but I wondered how many would bring in their papers next week.

"Get away from the window!" Officer Bill C. shouted to Dee.

She was near the door, looking through the window onto the visitors' room.

After they left, I asked him why he had said that.

"They are not allowed to look out the windows," he replied with no further explanation.

I made a mental note to find out what purpose this served, since there were windows in nearly every room. I thought that would be like working in a candy factory but not being able to eat the candy. Too much temptation for me to handle, I knew, and I wondered what the disciplinary action would be for looking out a window.

As I gathered my things from the classroom and entered the hallway, the fumes from the cafeteria made me want to throw up. I couldn't begin to imagine what was for dinner. I hurriedly got Marie to take me downstairs. When I reached the sidewalk, I began to dry heave as I ran to my car.

Once the fresh air had settled my stomach, I got into my car and sat there crying. I didn't realize what an emotional day it had been for me. I needed to review all that had happened in my sessions here.

Hear Our Voices

As I approached the lobby, hoping to graduate my first class of inmates, I felt anxious about whether or not the women had completed their assignments. I was also curious to know what they had written and how they expressed themselves.

I was nervous seeing the officer who had originally made me feel unwelcome. I gave him a friendly smile, but this time he seemed as cold as a fish. With an undertone that reminded me of his power, he questioned me about my license, visitor's pass and locker key.

I felt stunned and wanted to say, "Hey, it's me. The one you were so friendly to in my earlier visits. Don't you recognize my face or my voice?" I had learned, however, how important it was to remain polite and keep the conversation to the business at hand.

Marie appeared, smiling as usual. She informed me that Anne had decided not to start a new class until February. It was the beginning of January, and this meant I would continue with the same group for the next three weeks. I felt upset and was certain my face told all. I didn't appreciate being notified of a last-minute change with no explanation.

"Go with the flow," I told myself. "This is not the outside corporate world where negotiation is possible; it's prison."

As I prepared my music and personal sign-up sheet, an unfamiliar face appeared in the doorway and announced that she had registered for the new class. Rima, a young woman about five months pregnant, shook my hand. I told her apologetically that there was no new class until the beginning of February. She walked back to her unit looking disappointed, and I recognized a new set of circumstances that would challenge me.

When the women arrived, they handed me their papers on their way into class, much to my surprise and delight. Quietly, they sat in their spaces and waited for me to speak. What changes since the early weeks! I explained the adjustment in the schedule.

"We signed up for the next session," Atlanta and Jesse said proudly.

I handed them their certificates with a hug, and we all clapped as each woman received her diploma. They beamed from ear to ear. As we settled into the exercises, Atlanta stood up and asked me to read the papers.

"I'll read them at home," I answered.

"No, we want you to read them out loud," Atlanta persisted.

When I said I wouldn't read the individual names, the group chanted, "We want to hear the names."

I picked up the papers, some on long sheets, some on ripped pieces of paper, and one on a dinner napkin. I inhaled, feeling on the spot, but then I began to read.

"What I like about this class is it makes me feel good and relaxes my mind. The teacher brings peace among the women and touches our souls. I would appreciate it if this class would continue," wrote Atlanta.

Sue had underlined the words "Fitness Awareness Class" and neatly numbered her thoughts:

1) It helped my old broken leg a lot.

2) I am feeling good about myself more than ever before.

3) I love the teacher, and she has lots of patience with us. I hope she will be around on the outside when I get out so I can keep up my exercises. Thank You.

Choni wrote, "What I got out of my fit and awareness class was an opportunity to meet a wonderful lady, our teacher. I got to listen to meditation music and learn new exercises."

"What I enjoyed about the fit and wellness was how not in touch I was with certain parts of my body. How great to excite and exercise my body. And, that teacher, Ronnie, is a wonderful woman who enjoys her work and shares it with us. From your student, Cherie."

Shanee wrote, "The thing I liked about this class was the peace that was brought between us women, the solitude, the quiet time and brilliant aura around us. Our instructor has a lot of patience with us, and she is a beautiful person."

"What I got out of this class was calm and inner peace. These classes took me away from the life behind the wall for an hour. I think every inmate should be made to join. I know when I leave, my mind, body and soul feels much better. Peace, Twanda."

"The thing I likes most is that it brought me comfort. I had closed places I thought would never open. It gave me the ability to get in touch with my inner self. To conclude, I appreciate you taking time out of your life to be with us. Forever, Jeorgina."

While reading these papers, I felt such love from the women that I wanted to cry, and I told them so. What a gift of love!

After we completed class, I asked the ladies to tell Rima, the pregnant girl, she could join us for the two-week interim. Atlanta departed and reappeared with two more pregnant women. One was seven months along and the other looked about four months pregnant.

"I wanted you to tell them it's OK to come to class if you're pregnant," Atlanta said excitedly. She was becoming my agent.

Driving home, I couldn't wait to share these letters with my husband, with the world. My inner voice once again had put me on the right path. I knew I was meant to be working with women in prison.

Sliding into the Next Session

I was ending my second six-week session. I wondered where the time had gone. I watched the six ladies as they filed into the classroom and felt sad that two of them would probably be paroled soon. I wanted to share some very important thoughts.

Deolores, who had been with me from the beginning, informed me that she could stay only for half an hour, because she had just gotten a job in the kitchen. She would be helping to serve dinner.

The women can earn a small amount of monetary compensation, usually a dollar a day, and are given time off toward their sentences for completing programs such as creative writing, GED preparation, and computer programming, to name a few. They also have opportunities to sign up for prison chores such as cafeteria work, scrubbing floors, cleaning the restrooms, and working in the library.

"Sounds good to me," I told her. *I'd be signed up for everything that would hurry the process of parole,* I thought. I reminded myself that they did not have the socio-economic background or self-discipline that I had, and most of the women weren't motivated for the same reasons that I was. Often, in their home environments, their parents didn't work, but instead lived off welfare, slept until noon, and spent their social time talking about get-rich schemes.

One day, Gina told me that she would have to leave class thirty minutes early since she was having special out-of-town visitors. She seemed so excited. I wondered who was coming to see her. I was getting used to these class disruptions and tried to maintain my composure.

After thirty minutes of stretching, I decided to dedicate the next portion of class time to Christie and Mimie, since they would be released the following week. Where they lived and the people they associated with were crucial to their success. If they continued with the same habits that had brought them into prison, they would be most likely to return.

"It is important to remember what we talked about and the lessons we learned to support ourselves in times of weakness," I said. "Remember what I have told you, and this will help you through the tough times. Look for good, strong, positive support that you can rely on, as there will be times when you will start to be drawn into old patterns. Recognize them when they appear, and then *remember this group!*"

I found that all but one of the women in that class had children. They tended to hold on to the image of their children to get them through their time in jail. I wondered if the women realized how their behavior impacted these children. I thought of those visitors I saw weekly, with the little ones lined up to see their parents, getting exposed to prison at such an early age.

◆   ◆   ◆

"Is anything done about the holidays next week, Passover and Easter?" I asked the women.

"Probably nothing," Cherie said in a sad voice.

"I am certain religious services will be held in the chapel for all denominations," I answered, trying to sound upbeat.

Anne Riter and I then decided that perhaps adding an additional week between sessions (after the holidays) would be a good idea.

"There is a large group of ladies who have come into prison this week, and one is a college professor anxious to join the program," Anne said.

A college professor! I thought. She couldn't tell me why the inmates were incarcerated, but the inmates could speak of their crimes, and I wondered if the college professor would share. The women told me a lot about their families, addictions, and sometimes jobs, but only once had someone shared with me the crime that had landed her in prison. I wondered if it was hard for them to talk about their transgressions.

How many of these women had been victims of abuse, both sexual and physical, I wondered. When was the last time they really felt loved and supported in their lives? Not very often, perhaps. Perhaps never. I did recognize that they had brought me to a new depth of love and compassion. I felt as if I had been allowed to open my heart to places that I hadn't been able to reach before. I was grateful to these women for that gift.

◆   ◆   ◆

We began by sitting on the floor doing a forward bend, a great stretching exercise that lengthens the leg muscles and massages the internal organs. I noticed some of the women could easily touch their toes while some had difficulty touching their thighs.

"Hey girl, look at me, pretty good for fifty years old, ain't I?" Stephanie yelled.

"How about me for sixty-three?" I answered.

The startled look on her face said it all.

"You got to be shittin' me, girl," she replied.

The only reason I referred to my age was to let them know that a person can never be too old to start a healthy exercise regime. Letting your age not be a factor was a wonderful way to feel good about yourself and be more aware of your body's needs.

After our relaxing guided imagery, Stephanie shared with the class that she was looking forward to taking her sons apple picking in her bright red Corolla. She was to be released in a few weeks.

"My boys are with their old man, and I know he doesn't care about them. He only wants them monthly checks to take his girlfriend datin'," she said sadly. "I'm going to take them for barbecue chicken after we go apples pickin'. I got a favorite place in Dorchester that not too many people know about. Their sauce is bright red with a flavor only my momma can match."

◆ ◆ ◆

After the spring holidays and a week break, I began the third six-week series. I waited in the classroom for the new ladies to appear, wondering who would come through the door. I read the list of names and was surprised to find that there would be twelve. Atlanta appeared smiling at the door, followed by Rima, two familiar faces from my previous classes.

"I really need to be here for my baby. I want to have an easy time pushing this little creature out into the world," Rima explained.

As time went on, court dates dwindled the number of women down to about six or seven. Some of the women complained about their inertia.

"My meds make me tired, and I just want to sleep," Atlanta said.

This comment made me wonder for the first time how many of these women were medicated and why. I thought it best to explain again to the group the benefits of continuing to do these postures back in their cells throughout the week.

"Pick one or two postures from the class, practice daily, and you will begin to notice an increase in energy. Some of those aches and pains will start to disappear. Each week, I'll hear how much better you are starting to feel. I speak from my own experiences."

I felt this would be a perfect time to explain about energy, the yin and yang. This represents the male and female energies, and how when we are aware of our body's energies, we can work on balance and harmony within our own anatomical system. They appeared to be interested, listening quietly. I felt it would be important to give them some energizing postures to practice during the week.

I started with the woodchopper.

"Put your hands in prayer position, lifting them high and back over your head as you take in a deep breath, and bring your hands down to the floor while exhaling the sound, *HA*. Imagine you are chopping wood."

We continued this sequence nine times, faster each time. When we finished, some of the women said they were hot and wanted to take off their uniform shirts.

"That's not a good idea," said Atlanta.

"Them officers know that's not allowed. Let's keep it cool," Frances said.

I had them stand against the wall as support to do several leg exercises, and they all looked like ballerinas, which one of the ladies noted out loud. These women were really into their femininity, and that told me they would be open to more creative postures. I knew this class would be receptive to doing guided imagery, using their minds in a positive manner, which I was certain most of them had rarely experienced.

◆　　　◆　　　◆

I should be more aware of the high rates of Hepatitis B, AIDS and venereal diseases among women in prison, I thought in the middle of a class one day.

I had come from a traditional medical background, and awareness in the hospital was important, but I didn't want to dwell on these diseases and have it color my personal feelings toward my students. I had read several articles that said in women's prisons more than 50 percent of the inmates suffered from some form of mental illness.

All prisons had mental health professionals, but there were too few to cover the large number of mentally ill inmates, so little was done to treat the underlying disease. The correctional officers did receive training focused on suicide prevention, but not in-depth training on spotting symptoms of mental illness.

We had finished the exercise part of the session, and I did a brief meditation, bringing them into a state of total relaxation. This they really liked, and when we shared in the circle, they truly seemed like visionary women.

"I felt like I was a feather floating in the sky, oh so light," Cheryl said.

"I felt like I was everywhere, traveling the earth, over trees, up mountains and floating in the rivers. Such peace I have never known," Sara said, still looking spacey.

Today, Gina was leaving. I had the group members give her positive messages.

Her eyes welled up, and I knew in my heart she would not be back again. There were not many inmates who gave me this feeling, but Gina was one of them.

One day, Gina had come to class with bad menstrual cramps and asked if she could just participate in the meditation and relaxation time, which she did with her eyes closed, never moving. After that class, she had said quietly, "I feel better. Thank you for allowing me to stay."

She had been a good student and really wanted to continue doing this type of program outside. I told her that she could write me, care of the program director, and I would gladly answer. This was the only way former inmates could communicate with a teacher after they were paroled, and Gina was the only person I had encouraged to write. I felt my support would continue to be helpful for her.

Angel escorted me out that day and told me that I would probably not see her again, either. State cutbacks meant more layoffs. Usually seniority mandated when you were laid off, even if it meant the best person was dismissed.

The hospital where I had previously worked had used the same procedure. Right before I left, they were leaning toward a change that would keep the most competent person for the job, although who you knew in higher places would still take precedence over everything else.

I gave Angel a big hug and wished her well, thanking her for the support she had given me. She was very dedicated to helping the inmates with their social and personal problems and also did a lot to obtain support for them when they were released. I hoped she would return.

Cutbacks were common in most fields, but they seemed especially difficult when they happened in the penal system, where there may be 1500 prisoners and 500 guards. These 500 guards covered three shifts, seven days a week. When you broke the numbers down, there were five prisoners per guard, and the number of prisoners kept growing. We were really in a critical situation; more resources were needed both in personnel and in rehabilitation.

When I was young, I didn't know anyone in prison. Today, I often know someone directly or someone else I know knows someone who is incarcerated, perhaps even a member of the family. If conditions aren't improved, we will face riots and more lockdowns, as well as health issues. I am convinced that personnel in these institutions also need a mandatory relaxation and stress-reduction program on a monthly basis.

◆   ◆   ◆

I received two particularly inspirational papers from this class.

Cassandra wrote: "This program lets you relax from everything. It relaxes my body as well as my mind. When I come out of the class every Thursday, I feel mellow and nothing at all bothers me for the rest of the day. I just keep thinking about the class and what we did, such as listening to a guided soothing tape, hearing the contents of it makes you think of things that you wouldn't have thought of before. Listening, a word I never used in my life. It feels good to be able to stretch my body in different ways each week and feel alive. Where have I been for the past twenty-five years? Thank you."

Roma wrote: "I really enjoyed the class. It made my body feel relaxed and cleared my mind, flushing out all negativity. I would recommend it to anyone. I did not like that we didn't get enough time, but I enjoyed it a lot and appreciate your coming in at your time and helping us. I want to go to college; and when I am released, I will continue these exercises when trying to focus on my homework. Promise you'll continue to work with us."

In these letters, the women had often written about being able to express their feelings and learn techniques to relax their bodies, tools to take out into the world with positive support.

◆   ◆   ◆

Another Thursday had arrived. As I walked into the lobby, I felt amazed again at the large number of little ones there, escorted by young mothers. Occasionally, I saw several generations together. Often, I wasn't sure whether a woman was a child's mother or grandmother. As I waited for my new escort to take me upstairs, a woman sat next to me with a tiny baby, probably three or four weeks old with big brown eyes and a frail body. The baby whimpered until the mother produced a pacifier. I smiled at the little one and said a prayer that he or she might know some life other than prison.

◆   ◆   ◆

As I prepared for the last session of another six-week series, I called Anne to make sure the certificates were ready. Again, I heard pressure in her voice.

"There hasn't been any time to run off the graduation certificates, so make next week a free week and you can distribute them then. I promise they will be ready," Anne said.

Usually I ended the last class by giving each woman an opportunity to share her favorite postures or stretches. We listened to her instructions and all joined in. I started off with some preliminary head rolls and stretching, adding some shoulder rolls to release tension in the neck and shoulders. When I finished, the women demonstrated their favorites, and I observed how well they retained the exercises I had taught them. Some were proud of their new teaching skills.

This made me feel good, as they were willing to be open to new avenues of physically exploring their bodies and connecting with the body, mind and spirit.

Next, I asked them to lie on the floor to do a relaxing guided imagery. I decided to have them envision being at a beach, lying on the sand, and feeling the sun on their bodies at the edge of the water. I asked them to feel the waves slowly coming over their feet and enjoying the sensation of each wave. Then slowly, I guided them with the wave of warmth and relaxation going to every part of their bodies until they were in a total state of serenity: just breathing and relaxing. Slowly I had them open their eyes. I was amused that some women were snoring and not easily aroused.

As they began to bring their awareness back into the room, I asked them to stay connected with that feeling of peace and relaxation. When they were ready, I instructed them to sit up, and I gave them an opportunity to share how they felt. All of the women I've worked with were very imaginative and open to the metaphors I suggested.

I promised them that before we ended the class, I would do a little experiment on feeling their energy. They were eager, displaying excitement on their faces.

"Close your eyes and rub your hands briskly together," I instructed. "Now separate your hands slowly about one inch apart, palm to palm, and stop. Stop and feel the energy between your hands."

Next, we expanded to two inches, stopping to feel the energy, then expanding to four inches. We reverted back to the two inches and then one inch, pausing to feel the energy. They excitedly shared that they felt the energy between their hands. Some felt more at the greater distance and some more at the shorter distance.

Again, I had them close their eyes and hold hands in the circle, mentally sending the energy clockwise around our circle, feeling that energy, then stopping and reversing the flow of energy in a counter-clockwise direction. Finally, we stopped that flow and returned to letting our own energy move naturally.

"Open your eyes," I said. "How did that feel for you?"

Frances, Stephanie, and Alyce felt the direction to the left was stronger while Charlene, Deborah and the other women felt the direction to the right as stronger. They all agreed that when I said to stop the flow, they felt the lack of the energy.

This was a wonderful opportunity to introduce the women to their Human Energy Fields, or Human Aura, which was another way to connect with inner awareness. They were amazed at their results, and some said they would try it during the week with their roommates.

I talked about what happens when people get anxious, because I was aware of the high anxiety level with these women together twenty-four hours a day. I showed them that holding their breath created more anxiety, and in prison that anxiety most often lead to outbursts of anger.

"If you just take a moment to close your eyes, take a couple of breaths in and slowly exhale, you'll begin to return to a normal state of consciousness, and you'll be better equipped to handle the situation that caused your state of anxiety."

I glanced at my watch, noting that I had five minutes left, and then turned to Deborah and asked her to share what her plans were when she left prison. Deborah had done exceptionally well these six weeks, and I hoped she'd continue when she left.

I hadn't expected her to do so well, given the way things had started for her in the class. She had begun with the previous group but had bowed out. "This ain't for me," she had said and made a quick exit. She had been in prison twice before for working the streets and selling drugs. But since then, she had vowed never to return to that lifestyle because she had been diagnosed with AIDS.

She reiterated that point on her last day with us but added no further information about living with AIDS. Instead she said, "I never married, but once was very much in love; it didn't work out." She looked at the floor.

"What is your passion?" I asked.

"I don't understand, please explain what you mean by passion," she said. Before I could speak, her face lit up and she shouted, "My mother!"

Deborah said that during all the things she did in her life, both good and bad, her mother had always been there for her.

"This time I am going to make her my passion," she continued. "I am going to live with my mother and begin to lead a life that will make my mother proud of me."

We applauded her. Stephanie gave a whistle through her teeth. I nervously waited for the program officer to rush in, since class ran a few minutes over. We ended class on a high.

◆   ◆   ◆

A week of R and R was really looking good. I was tired and eagerly awaiting a vacation in Florida with my husband. Time off was when new, creative ideas flowed, and I could implement those ideas in my programs. The weather would be lovely in April as the Florida sun becomes strong, warm and not yet humid, with a few scattered showers to nourish the plants and trees.

Unfortunately, only two days after we settled in, my sister-in-law died suddenly. My husband flew home immediately. Thirty-six hours later, I followed to be with him and comfort the family.

My husband and his family are Jewish, so traditionally they sit *shivah*. It is a mourning period of seven days after the funeral when family and friends come to the home and pay their respects. This is done after the burial services, because Jewish tradition calls for burial within twenty-four hours of death.

I liked this tradition. It seemed more compassionate than going to the funeral parlor, passing through a line murmuring, "I'm sorry," or "my sympathies to you and your family," followed by a time sitting in a chair and gawking at all those in line until you are bored and feel your dutiful time is up. I always forget to sign the guest book until I'm exiting and then look to see if there are any names I recognize. I suppose the family uses the book to see who came and who didn't.

I wondered how an inmate would attend a funeral service. Do they arrive in shackles, accompanied by a guard and in their prison uniform? What were the rules regarding prisoners attending the funeral of a loved one?

Picturing this scene in my mind reminded me of yet another loss of privileges when imprisoned.

PART II
The Women

Prelude

Since the first six-week class, I have worked with many women in prison. Several inmates made an impact on my life and helped me to express my feelings openly. I had never revealed my private life in public, but through my connections with these women, I was able to open up parts of myself that I previously protected, fearing that I would be harshly judged. After struggling with these feelings, I was able to move forward and present myself in a more honest and open way.

Each of these women, Cecily, Sui, Luvell, Atlanta, Ebony, and Mimie, represented a piece of me. I may not have been incarcerated, but I had periods in my life when I felt imprisoned.

Their stories seemed to reflect parts of my own life.

Like Luvell, who was pregnant while in jail, I felt trapped when I became pregnant with my third child while in a suffocating marriage.

Like Cecily, who wanted to be loved and to feel safe, I longed to be genuinely loved as a child and as a wife.

Like Sui, who explored the world of drugs with a questionable boyfriend, I, too, kissed a lot of frogs before I found my prince.

Like Atlanta, who mothered all her friends in jail and became "my agent," I often neglected to nurture myself.

Like Ebony and Mimie, whose families set high standards for achievement, I felt a lot of pressure from my family to succeed in academics, from my previous husband to support him and the children, and from the internal pressures I placed on myself to be an overachiever in whatever I did.

Cecily, Sui, Luvell, Mimie, Ebony, and Atlanta stand out in my memory, but many others were important to my experience as well. I am grateful to all the women with whom I worked and for the opportunity to have been a part of their lives, if only for a brief time.

Sui

I met Sui when I was relatively new in the system, with my second group of students. Anne Riter told me about this new inmate, a graduate of Harvard Business School. She was fresh from her court sentence and still in a state of shock and denial. Anne encouraged Sui to sign up for my Fit and Wellness program.

"She would benefit from your class. You could be a good influence in her life," Anne said.

She looked at me across her desk, which was piled high with papers, "I've heard from the inmates that the relaxation techniques are beneficial. Some are sleeping more soundly, and others say they feel less stress, particularly around family issues."

While riding the elevator to the eleventh floor, I wondered what Sui would look like, conjuring up an image of a thin Asian gal in her twenties, looking very studious behind thick glasses. How receptive would she be to my program?

As I entered the classroom to prepare for my new group, I wondered about all twelve ladies who had signed on for this series: their sizes, shapes, and personalities, and the intrigue they would each bring with them.

The great thing about the Fit and Wellness program was that most of the women were receptive to it and enjoyed coming to class. It wasn't usually a problem to fill the roster. I preferred to have only twelve participants, because the classroom was small. They spread the word to their fellow inmates about how good they felt and about the positive effects from the relaxation exercises they did. A larger number would have been difficult to control, because some would try to use the time for mindless chatter and group distractions. These classes often combined women from both units, so it gave them a chance to catch up on cross-unit gossip. It reminded me of being a teacher in the movie *Blackboard Jungle.*

"Hello," "excuse me" and "shhh" went unnoticed, but one ring of my Tibetan bells usually brought them to attention. I always reminded a new group about the rules of the bells; if I rang them twice for someone's misbehavior, that woman was dismissed from class.

I stepped into the classroom, turned on the flute music they said was so relaxing, and in walked Sui. She fit my profile of a Harvard honors graduate: thick glasses over dark eyes, small frame, and snow-white skin accented by black hair. She wore a rosary around her neck, which amused me.

Some who were here for the first time found religion again. Catholics wore the rosary to give them strength to overcome their addictive habits. When they got out of jail, that inspirational rosary often got relegated to the drawer, not to be seen or used until the next trip back to jail. Religion was one of the available supports, and God by many names didn't go away. They tried desperately to find light in the darkness. Other clergy were often present to share their teachings with the women. There were many women who claimed to be Baptist and attended weekly services, singing and preaching the word of God to the prison congregation.

A friend of mine, Father George, had been a prison chaplain for eight years. He told me that when inmates first came to prison, they spent a lot of time reading the Bible, attending Sunday services, and saying the rosary. As time went on, the didn't read the Bible as often, and they didn't always wear the rosary around their necks. They did normally continue to attend Mass to get away from their units.

Sui's blue uniform told me that she was in the recovery unit and had been caught selling or buying drugs, or possibly abused alcohol. I wondered what her parents thought, as I thought certainly she had to be the first one in her family to be incarcerated.

At first, Sui was shy. She did everything she was told and had obviously been a very good student. I could imagine why some of the inmates were here from their demeanor, but she didn't reveal any clues about who she was, not with body language, mannerisms, or speech. Her appearance was neat, she spoke only when someone talked to her, and she answered in one or two words only.

Sui concentrated on doing the exercises perfectly. She seemed inscrutable. Each week she paid attention to the yoga postures and engaged in the positions more skillfully than anyone else in the class. Sometimes her skill seemed to exceed mine. Sui did forward and backward bends as perfectly as the yogis.

"You must have done these exercises before," Naomi observed.

"I ain't ever seen anyone bend like a pretzel," Suzanna added.

Sui merely smiled.

After the exercises, during the third class, I instructed the group to visualize, imagine, or be aware of a place that brings comfort and peace.

"Really look at your surroundings, and imagine that you are now in that place of total peace. Visualize someone who loves and supports you in your life. Welcome that person with love," I said softly. "Tell him or her how grateful you are for their love and support, and spend a few moments talking to that person about your life, describing the support you need at this particular time. Speak from your heart."

I paused for a few minutes, allowing them time to engage in this imagery. Then, I gently brought their awareness back to the room.

"Wiggle your hands and feet, slowly open your eyes and sit up in the circle," I said. I asked for volunteers to share their experience from this meditation.

Sui was the first to speak. Her voice, pitched an octave above her usual range, betrayed her anxiety, "I was on a mountaintop having sex with my boyfriend, and it felt so liberating." She gave a slight giggle.

I waited for more, but that was all she said.

Each one is like a surprise package, I thought. *You can't always guess what is inside.*

◆   ◆   ◆

I liked to have structure in my classes, so I always began by having each woman share what was on her mind. I encouraged them to talk about the kind of week they were having and to express feelings of stress. After venting their emotions, they seemed more focused. It helped to keep their minds from wandering and their mouths from chattering. Most were serious about the program and acted annoyed if distracted by idle chatter.

Sui had completed the six-week course and opted to stay for the next six weeks, which pleased me. I suggested to her at the end of the first session that the exercises would be a way for her to stay connected with her feelings and an excellent support system to use after she was paroled. She listened intently and nodded her head but didn't speak. I hoped that I had planted a seed.

As usual, I asked the women to write how the program benefited them at the end of the six-week session. Sui intrigued me by what she wrote. I imagined that she must have prepared it as if she were writing a term paper. Her feelings were scattered over many pages: "I really enjoyed this class. This class seems to have a deep yoga influence. I am now able to have some tools to clear my mind from stress and tension that occur during the day. This was my first attempt at meditation. I found it very calming and relaxing. I have begun to use it at bedtime when my mind starts to race over the past events that brought me here. I would teach this to my boyfriend."

"I can't believe this has happened to me," she said after that last class. "I was numb when the judge ordered me to jail."

I sensed from her withdrawn attitude that she still felt a lot of denial and fear.

◆　　　◆　　　◆

Halfway through Sui's second six-week class, she confided in me that she expected an early parole.

"Don't tell the rest of the class in case it doesn't materialize," she said in a low tone. "Never count on the initial date set for parole—it usually doesn't happen," Sui confided. This kind of situation occurred often. A date would be set for early release, only to have it changed because the necessary papers or release forms had not been signed or properly sent to all the appropriate channels and stamped for approval. Sometimes it was because the home situation hadn't passed inspection as a positive support system. There were yards of red tape to wade through before release day. So it was a waiting game.

Sui emphasized again the need to be secretive.

"I don't want to jinx my chances. I will know for certain next week the exact day and will be happy to tell the group my good news then," she said.

"Please keep me informed so the class and I have an opportunity to say good-bye."

She nodded.

I left class that afternoon wondering where she would go and what her plans were after parole. Sui intrigued me.

◆　　　◆　　　◆

Another Thursday came. As I fought mid-afternoon traffic on the expressway, I thought about Sui, wondering if this would be her last class. Would she take anything from her incarceration that would have a positive effect on her life outside? I thought that her boyfriend would play an important part in her life, but I wasn't sure he would exert a positive influence.

I'll never know, and perhaps that is best.

The class marched in looking like soldiers, quite a contrast to their usual uncoordinated arrival. I wondered if there had been disciplinary action in the unit. I wanted to ask, but I knew prison rules didn't allow me to violate their privacy.

Sui was the first to enter. She whispered that these were definitely her last two days. I asked if we could tell the class so that we could send her off with some positive messages. She nodded and smiled.

We went through the usual circle sharing. When I told the ladies Sui would be leaving on Friday, there was a murmur of response.

"Lucky you."

"I wish it were me."

I suggested that we go around the circle and give Sui a supportive farewell.

"Don't let yourself come back here again," Stacey advised her.

"Remember how bad it was in here when you start to give in to your old habits," Naomi said.

"Thank you for being such a positive influence and helping us read and fill out those release forms," Mary added. "May God keep you strong and away from here."

"Amen!" the women chorused as they clapped their hands.

I knew they spoke from the heart; I wanted to cry. I felt the sincerity in their messages.

After class, Sui waited until the others had disappeared down the hall. She presented me with a dove that she had drawn on a card. Beneath the bird she had written PEACE in big blue letters.

Cecily

Cecily, who was my vocal lady, would prance into the classroom with an "I'm in charge" attitude. She loved to talk about her family life and took every opportunity to do so. When we did our sharing, I would often have to direct her to stop so we could move on to the next person or ask for her silence when I was ready to begin the class. Each week I felt her opening up a little more about her experience of life in prison. She told stories in a way that held me spellbound. None of the other women had been as forthcoming about prison life as she was.

Cecily was a heavy-set woman, mostly because she ate junk food in the canteen in the evening. She said that the institution got the prisoners hooked on coffee and sweets from the canteen, then took it away from them one week every month.

I asked her what she meant, and she said, "They only let the units have access to the canteen three weeks out of the month." Before I could ask why, Cecily was off on another subject, and class was ready to begin.

The women with addictions had an exceptionally hard time with caffeine and sugar removal, and many of them complained about headaches and jitteriness. It was drug withdrawal.

Cecily's skin was a coffee color, freckled everywhere. She had beautiful, thick lips, and when she spoke, she revealed a magnificent set of ivory teeth. She wore her shoulder-length, mousy brown hair in a fifties look, pushed back and tightly turned over in a roll across the back of her head. Not one strand of hair was ever out of place. I often wondered how her hair held that roll so securely; barrettes and hairpins were not allowed.

Cecily was in for crimes related to alcohol and gambling addictions. When her gambling got out of control, she forged checks to place bets on sporting events, buy scratch cards and make frequent trips to the casinos. She had stayed clean for seven years before this incarceration, her second. She had once had a good job as an LPN in a nursing home and enjoyed taking care of older folks.

Cecily talked openly one afternoon in class about having been raped by a boyfriend. He used to tie her to the bedposts and perform demanding sexual acts on her.

"I cried inwardly, because he put a washcloth in my mouth," she said.

After he was finished, he shouted obscenities at her, and then untied her.

"Most of the time, I tried to keep my eyes closed and imagine I was in the sky, flying like a bird."

I wanted to ask her many questions about who her boyfriend was and how long she had been with him, but I needed to respect her space. I learned to be a good listener.

Her son John, a responsible young man, worked in the computer industry. He lived with her in a small house in the suburbs. John took care of her house and paid all the bills. She said he lectured her about her habits of excessive gambling and drinking.

"I pretend I don't hear him. When I was in those drinking moods, I'd listen to no one. I had all the right answers," she said. "I would get mad and start to beat him up."

John would leave and stay at a friend's house for a couple of days until Cecily became sober and sorrowful and called him to say, "I'm sorry. Come home."

She would promise to go to AA.

One day, the police knocked on her door to arrest her for check forgery.

"The saddest day of my life was when I was handcuffed and driven off to jail—a place I vowed *never* to return to after my first incarceration," she said.

Cecily had six months to go by the time she started my class, and she tried very hard to get her sentence reduced. She worked in the cafeteria and the library. Unfortunately, Cecily's outbursts of rage sent her to "the hole" for fighting with her cellmates or speaking disrespectfully to the officers. She visited the hole about three times a month.

After attending my program, she began to lose weight, and her visits to the hole became less frequent. Following every class, she would update me on her progress. She was proud of her accomplishments, and I encouraged her. I saw her self-esteem begin to grow.

Cecily took pride in faithfully attending all of the classes she had signed up to take. Previously she would start a program and then not finish it, saying that she was tired or had menstrual cramps. Those were her two favorite excuses. But she really wanted to get out of jail and start a new life. She learned that the skills she gained in the program could be utilized on the outside when life started to get out of control. I gave her names of places in her area where she could sign up for meditation and relaxation classes, hoping she would follow through on the suggestions.

I wondered where I might see Cecily next. I saw her move from the GP to recovery unit and back to the GP unit. The inmates initially could choose where they were assigned, space permitting. If they were in for an addictive problem, they could request to be placed in the recovery unit. If they were in denial about an addiction and not ready for rehabilitation, they were housed in the GP unit. A woman in the recovery unit who was not doing her twelve-step programs would be sent to the GP unit. The women couldn't move back and forth at whim. There was only one initial opportunity to be part of the recovery unit and their programs. At first, I was confused as I observed Cecily traveling from unit to unit until one of the officers explained the system. I haven't seen many in my class make these switches.

Meet the Pregnant Mamas

After six months of teaching, I had become a familiar face associated with the prison programs. My "agent," Atlanta, introduced me to several pregnant mamas for March's class. I cautioned them to modify the postures to suit the various stages of their condition.

"If any of these exercises feel uncomfortable, don't do them," I said.

I noticed that Sheline wasn't paying attention. She was busy making comments to Georgine about how stretching wasn't good for the well-being of her baby. I asked her to share her concerns with the whole class.

"I'm in my seventh month, third pregnancy, and it's a girl," Sheline informed the group. "I had two miscarriages. Some spotting in my first three months this time, but the doctor said all is well. My boyfriend will be mad at me if I lose another one," she said in a surly tone. "He likes to see what those sperms are doin'."

"Are you sure you want to be in this class?" I asked.

"Don't know why I signed up. Probably 'cause Atlanta said it was fun," she replied.

I made a mental note to tell Anne Riter that Sheline was too pregnant to be in the class. I didn't need to be accused of causing a miscarriage.

Luvell announced she was six months pregnant. She walked over and shook my hand, a strong, deliberate handshake. I felt power radiating from this beautiful black woman who absorbed every word of mine with her big brown eyes. I wondered what she was doing in jail.

Cassandra was back, having had a rough two weeks in lockdown. She promised she would continue to come, as she liked the way class relaxed her. Cassandra was four months pregnant, a bundle of nervous energy and easily agitated. She frequently assaulted her roommates and ended up in lockdown.

◆   ◆   ◆

This was such a unique group—a blend of pregnancies, miscarriages and those having and those not wanting children. Mariel, another newcomer, joined the group. She was older, perhaps in her forties, with several scars on her face and her left arm. They looked like old knife wounds that I had seen on patients in the emergency room. I welcomed her, and she shared that this was her second time in jail. This time Mariel had opted not to take an early release, as she was too scared to go back into society. An inmate in the recovery unit, she expressed a strong desire to stay clean. She had just miscarried, sharing no other information about her pregnancy.

"I can't live with any of my family; that's where all my troubles start. I need a place of my own, away from the temptations that brought me back in jail. My daddy can't stop sellin' and I can't stop buyin'," Mariel said. "This time I ain't going near him with his rolls of money and goodies to sniff."

Genie, from the recovery unit, who couldn't handle stress, entered.

"I have a lot of pain in my neck and shoulders," she said. "I was addicted to medical drugs, not them recreational drugs. I need to work through the pain without using drugs."

A second-time offender, she was eager to use all the tools available for a healthier lifestyle. "My goal is to be drug free and start a family," she informed the class.

Stephanie, a beautiful black-haired woman, had participated in the previous session. "I'm looking forward to getting out of this joint and taking my triplet sons, Adam, Bob and Carl, to the Franklin Park Zoo. They talk about seein' the animals when I come home. Can't disappoint them no more."

Regis, a scrawny black woman, who I'd seen around the halls and in the elevator, was often being escorted to the hole. Her abdomen was distended, and her eyes were yellow, which told me that she had liver disease.

Regis refused to sit with the group. "If this is about diet, I'm needing to gain weight, not lose it. I'm out of here!" she exclaimed loudly.

She marched out saying, "And no kids for me." I was frustrated, because she left without giving me an opportunity to explain the program. I understood why she was in the hole more than in her cell.

Camille, a tall, slender beauty who was only about eighteen years old, knocked on the door and rushed in, out of breath. She shook my hand, apologized for being late and explained that she needed to have blood drawn, because she was a diabetic and four months pregnant. It was Camille who stopped me after the third class to say that she felt intimidated by two of the women in the class.

"Who are they?" I asked, already picturing who sat next to her.

"Stephanie and Mariel are making remarks about how I can't stretch as far as they can. They giggle and imitate me," she said with her head down and her arms behind her back.

"I may not be back next week," she said sheepishly as she walked across the room to leave.

I offered to speak with the women, but she shook her head. "I don't need more trouble," she said.

I decided to take the situation to Anne Riter. I explained to Anne how Camille felt about the snide remarks from Stephanie and Mariel, which were made in an undertone so I couldn't hear them; otherwise I would have addressed the women in class. Anne assured me she would handle the situation discreetly so there would be no further comments. Anne had a special way of dealing with the women, bringing resolution to problems that occurred in her programs. At the next class, the women apologized for their behavior before we started to exercise. I knew there would be no more undertones.

Luvell

I noticed Luvell had positioned herself in the classroom right under the window so that she could focus on me and my instructions to the class. She reflected many years of hard living and now faced another crossroads in her life: she was about to give birth, with six months of her sentence to complete. She slowly lifted her blue prison shirt, revealing her pregnant, brown belly, and then abruptly lowered her shirt.

I looked at her quizzically.

"I'm hot, and this was a little fannin' for me and my baby," she said softly.

She knew the prison rules forbade inmates to expose any part of their bodies to personnel or fellow inmates. She dared to bend the rules.

As I left class, I had unsettled feelings about the shirt incident and decided to reread the manual that outlined rules and regulations for the inmates. There have been a few occasions when I bent the rules. I let them look out the window to see who the visitors were for the afternoon, which is a no-no, for instance.

I liked to remind my classes that being here was easier than going out in the streets.

Prison is relatively safe, because it is away from the environment that brought them to jail, and its structured programs help them master addictions, schooling, and parenting. I encouraged them to use jail time as a retreat and take the opportunity to sign up for all the classes that were offered.

"This is a time for reflection about *you*, to learn who *you* are and where *you* want to go from here," I frequently reminded them.

They listened and had good intentions, but I think they needed a strong will and determination to succeed. For most of the women, recovery would require moving out of their surroundings and away from the destructive relationships that had brought them to jail.

After being with Luvell for a few weeks, I noticed that she was the last one to leave and would always give me a big hug.

"God bless you, and thank you for caring," she would say.

I felt cautious about accepting her apparent gratitude. I had sometimes been dead wrong about people I thought I'd figured out.

◆　　　◆　　　◆

The weeks marched on, and Luvell continued to position herself at the same place in the classroom so that she could look directly into my eyes. I wondered what was going through her mind. I didn't always feel comfortable in her presence. Luvell had been a professor of political science at a prestigious college. She often talked about how smart and how talented she was and, above all, why she didn't belong in jail.

The manual confirmed that inmates were not allowed to expose themselves to other inmates, social workers, officers, volunteers or visitors at any time. Yet Luvell had exposed her skin in class more than once, including the time when she explained to me that she was fanning her baby. I had been trying to ignore her occasional exposures throughout the course. She did it some weeks and not others. Was it a case of raging hormones that set off a hot flash? I decided to bend the rule a little, unless others followed her example.

Luvell told me that for her prenatal care, she had been sent to a Boston hospital for monthly visits, during which she received a supply of vitamins and other supplements. After the baby's birth, he would be taken from her and go either to family members or foster care until Luvell's release. She might choose adoption for the baby, but she confided in me that she desperately wanted to keep him. Her two teenage daughters were with family members who weren't anxious to take on the burden of an additional child.

I asked about her mother. Luvell said she really never knew her mother, a drug addict, who dropped Luvell off at her grandmother's home when she was eight years old.

Her grandmother, a very spiritual person, attended church services every Sunday and volunteered as a neighborhood missionary proclaiming the need to *feel Jesus Christ in your heart* by attending the First Baptist Church and being *saved!*

"She truly was an advocate for living the spiritual life," Luvell said. "Sometimes the church would be filled with about forty new families that Nana Grace had recruited during the week. She always took me wherever she went and made sure I was clothed and well fed and did my school time. With all the good she radiated toward me, I still had a longing to see my mother."

Her mother was in and out of prison for drugs, prostitution, and living on the streets from state to state. Tears trickled down the sides of Luvell's face as she spoke. "I'm just like her; the very thing I promised my grandmother I wouldn't be."

I felt overcome with emotion but needed to maintain my poise.

"Luvell, you don't have to follow her path," I said. "You have a free will and an opportunity to make a new life for yourself and your new baby. This is your crossroads. Don't set yourself up for more disappointments. Imagine how your daughters are feeling about being shifted to different families while you are in prison!"

She said nothing. Still crying softly, she gave me the weekly hug and went to dinner. I wondered how much of an impact I made on her life. I wondered how I affected the lives of all the women. The only ones I ever saw again were repeat offenders who were returned to my class.

Of the two hundred women in the prison, about seven were then pregnant; most from the recovery unit. The percentage of pregnant women in the average prison population was 3 percent.

If babies born in prison tested positive for fetal drug and alcohol syndrome, they underwent additional blood tests and were closely monitored for withdrawal symptoms. The mothers were tested periodically during pregnancy for any trace of drugs.

◆   ◆   ◆

During my fourth week with Luvell, I noticed that she was looking out the window and not paying attention to my instructions.

"Please join us, Luvell. Are you feeling okay?" I asked.

"My Nana Grace is dying in the hospital, and here I sit," she replied.

"Doing these exercises and meditation will help you relax and reduce your stress level. If you would prefer to go back to your room, you have permission to leave," I said.

I didn't want her moodiness to begin to affect the group. She hesitated, then began to do the stretching. I felt she wanted to draw attention to herself and her life. They were there to support each other, but every woman experienced her own, personal journey.

I was more than halfway through the fifth class when Luvell arrived, sat down and positioned herself with the group. I hesitated to stop the class and question her tardiness. I thought after class would be a more appropriate time to review rules with her.

After the relaxation, Luvell sat up and started crying quietly.

"What's troubling you?" I asked.

"My Nana Grace passed away this morning, and that was my last hope for survival," she said. "My tower of strength is gone."

I asked each of the women to form a circle around her and extend their sympathies and support.

"I am truly sorry for your loss and will pray for her. I know how much she meant to you," Alicia said.

"I live with my grandma," Genie said, "and she puts up with all the troubles I give her. I'm in here for the second time, and I promised her I wouldn't be back. Seeing how sad you are makes me wanna cry for your Nana and mine. God bless you."

"If you want to talk in the canteen tonight, come sit with us," some of the women added.

These women truly felt her pain. It connected them with their own feelings about loss and abandonment. Silence prevailed for a few moments until Bill C. knocked on the door for dinner.

As Luvell was the last to leave, I gave her a hug.

"I will remember you and your Nana in my weekly healing circle," I said.

She smiled with gratitude.

Luvell decided to continue with the next six-week program, but as the weeks continued, she became less involved. She was attentive but somewhat withdrawn. I wondered what she thought as those final weeks of her pregnancy came to an end. She would be in the hospital for two days and then sent back to prison. Her family had decided to take the baby until she was paroled. Luvell said she had no home when she got out but would enter a halfway house, which would give her time to explore housing, find a job and get to know her baby.

The majority of the women finished out their time at a halfway house. This gave them freedom to research jobs, housing and plans for release. If they violated prison rules, they went back to jail.

In the fourth week of the next six-week segment, I was surprised to find Luvell absent. Some of her friends told me she was at the hospital and in labor. The medical people had decided to induce labor since she was spotting and because her water broke early.

◆　　◆　　◆

A new class brought an abundance of women, and I felt cramped for space. Since Anne Riter was on vacation, Elizabeth Khorn, the director of programs for men and women, had posted the sign-up sheet in all units. I watched in awe as the room kept getting smaller and smaller.

I noticed that Luvell didn't come, and I inquired as to her condition.

"She is recovering and needing to rest. She told us she had lots of stitches and is feeling mighty sore," Dora said.

After class I began walking toward the cafeteria to get the officer to send the elevator up for me. I felt a tap on my shoulder and turned to see Luvell.

"Why wasn't my name on the sign-up sheet?" she whispered. "I never saw that sign-up sheet."

I told her she was welcome to come to class but had to have Anne Riter's approval.

"I'll be at the next class. Maybe I'll get some of my energy back," she said.

She rolled her eyes and looked off into space as if a thousand miles away. I wondered if she would show up.

"No," my inner voice responded.

The weeks passed, and when I inquired about Luvell, her friends just shrugged their shoulders.

"She's taking a shower," Lee added.

I understood the message—no more Luvell. I wondered if she despaired, having lost her grandmother. Perhaps she was experiencing postpartum depression.

Atlanta

I'd been teaching the program for over two years and was pleased with how well the classes were received.

Atlanta was on my mind, because I had not seen her in a over a year. Occasionally, I asked one of the inmates if they had heard from her.

"No," or "She's gettin' out soon," was always the answer.

I felt sad about the possibility of Atlanta being paroled. Even though I no longer saw her, she was still recruiting women for my class.

Atlanta had been my first supporter of the Fit and Wellness program. She had told the women in her unit how great a class I had and encouraged them to sign up. I used to call her "my agent."

Although for a large woman, she weighed over 300 pounds, wore her uniform neatly, and slicked back her shiny hair. She was always smiling. I said if they were giving out awards, she would have received one for "Miss Congeniality." Everyone loved her. She took time to hear problems and gave advice and support.

When I was nervous and anxious in my first class, Atlanta attempted to do all the stretching exercises I taught. It wasn't easy for her, but it gave the other women an incentive to try, and it sure made my job easier as a teacher. The women seemed to follow her example; stretching and bending and doing the relaxation exercises. She was a good role model.

I knew that when she had entered jail, her first placement had been in the recovery unit. Several months into her recovery program, Atlanta wanted to be moved to the GP unit.

"I have more friends down there," she said.

She was transferred and continued to take her anti-depressants and seizure medicine. This made her sometimes too lethargic to attend class. I began to notice a decline in her attendance toward the end of the third session. She missed most of the fourth-session classes, sending one of the women up to tell me she was too tired. A couple of times, I overheard some of the women say that Atlanta was overmedicated.

I used to tell Atlanta that she would be perfect doing nails, gossiping with her clients and making them feel good about themselves and their lives. She smiled and said that sounded better than working the streets. I assumed she was letting me know that prostitution had brought her to prison.

Atlanta was the only one in class who owned her own house. Each week she would give me a tidbit about her home: the garden was her favorite place. She loved to plant tulips in the early spring and was sad she wouldn't be home to plant them this year. The next week, she would talk about her kitchen and how bright it was with its color scheme of blue, white, and orange. The kitchen had an oversized oven and lots of cabinet space for her cooking supplies.

"That's where I do my creating," she said. "I love to cook and follow my grandmama's recipes from the South." Smacking her lips, she added, "Spicy and hot are my motto."

The class all followed with a "yum."

Atlanta approached me during the last class. "I've been talking to my husband and asked him if we could turn our basement into an exercise room," she said.

I was both elated and shocked at how seriously she clearly took the program.

Her husband had agreed to call a few of his friends who did carpentry and see if they would come over to view the possibilities for building her an exercise room. "Then all you ladies can come to my house after you are out," she said with pride. "Even you, Ms. Ronnie, are welcome!"

I smiled and thanked her, knowing in my heart that it would be impossible to pay her a visit. The rules of the facility are that volunteers cannot associate with inmates either inside the facility or after they have left. I was not about to break those rules.

I often wondered if Atlanta followed through on her dream, though. I truly felt I had lost a friend when she left my class and returned to the outside world.

I hoped someone would take her place, but there was no one I felt I could rely on to bring in more women.

Ebony

In the circle of women, the beautiful one was Ebony, named after the magazine for black men and women. Her parents hoped that she would appear as a model on the cover. Her mother had high expectations for her as a child. Ebony always felt pressured to be number one. In school, she was expected to bring home all As. She was a natural when it came to singing, and she tried out for all the shows in high school. When she didn't get the lead roles, her mother would rush to school, wanting to know why her daughter had not been chosen. Ebony was embarrassed by these outbursts, because the students would make derogatory remarks to her. She spent most of her junior year at home because of depression. Ebony missed out on the junior prom, had no friends and lived a life behind closed doors. She was homeschooled and continued to excel in all her studies under pressures to succeed.

In her senior year, back at school, she developed the wrong kind of relationships. Ebony felt her newfound friends were cool, and they accepted her. She was introduced to pot, as a "relaxer." In the next couple of years, her pot habit transformed into a full-blown heroin addiction. Desperate for money to maintain her habit, she started working the streets. During a sting operation, she and her girlfriend were hauled into jail. Her family disowned her.

Of her time in jail, Ebony said, "The first time, I didn't care where I was. I only thought about my next fix."

She couldn't wait until she was free "to get me that high. No rehab for me."

"This second time," Ebony said in a somber voice, "has been enough of a descent into hell to make me want to stay as far away from drugs and anyone associated with them as I can."

She was to be released in two months and had been taking courses in preparation for college.

"Will you see your parents when you are paroled?" I asked.

Ebony hung her head and cried softly. I continued with class, not wanting to pressure her.

Ebony completed the six weeks and seemed excited to receive her certificate. She was a natural with the exercises and said she practiced daily.

"She sure does, first thing in the mornin', at afternoon recess, and again at bedtime," Ruby, one of her friends, said. "She's driving me nuts with the pressure she puts on herself to be always in one of them yoga positions."

I wondered what would happen to this talented and beautiful young woman.

I got nervous when Ruby said the forbidden word "yoga," but I decided silence was golden.

Mimie

After finally finding a parking space in an overcrowded lot and running five minutes behind schedule, I hurried across the street past two officers blowing smoke my way and quickly entered the lobby to sign in for my weekly class. Leaning against one of the two white pillars at the entrance to the jail was Mimie Rump, one of my former students. I was delighted to see her, and I impulsively gave her a hug.

Here she was in a pair of new, dark blue jeans and a vivid red-collared shirt hidden under a gray sweatshirt. Her bright white sneakers were tied perfectly in double knots. Mimie was holding a large, brown paper bag that I imagined might have contained her toothbrush, toothpaste neatly rolled, letters, drawings from the kids and grandkids to take home, the residue of her second time in jail.

Mimie looked heavier than when I had last seen her in the brown, two-piece, baggy uniform, which doesn't let anyone get a look at true body contour.

The uniforms reminded me of when I went to parochial school. We wore unflattering uniforms: shapeless, loose, navy, gabardine jumpers and white, starched shirts with only the collar and sleeves revealed, and knee socks or nylons with anklets and white bucks. They were meant to repress any sexual fantasies the boys might have.

"Is this the big parole day?" I asked her.

She grinned and said, "It's P-day. I am going home to enjoy my family. I enrolled for advanced computer classes. My social worker has gotten me some job interviews and things are looking real posi-

tive." She held in her hand a thick brown booklet of rules and regulations for parolees.

I shook her hand and wished her well as I continued toward the
front desk to sign in. I still wondered what type of parole violation
had brought her back to jail in the first place.

A New Perspective on a Haunting Memory

One man belongs in this section of women, because my contact with women in prison gave me a different perspective on my relationship with him.

I admired the women for talking openly about relationships with their husbands, boyfriends, and partners. Most of the women seemed to have made unwise choices and lost their identities. They became battered women, or battered their husbands, or gave up their own power, and became subservient to their mates.

Under the romantic influence of her boyfriend, Sui had joined his life of drugs. Cherie was frank about her prostitution and living under the control of a pimp. Cecily did everything to please her man, just to keep him in her life.

Hearing their stories brought back my own memories about dating a judge who had me under his control.

I was living in a small coastal town in Massachusetts, when a friend of mine, Jared Holmes, a detective at the courthouse, introduced Tim to me.

"You are perfect for him," Jared said. "Tim has expressed many times an interest in settling down and wanting to start a family."

I felt that finally this could free me from the horrific life I had experienced in my marriage and the uncertainties and loneliness of life as a single mother. The opportunity to be a stay-at-home mother and wife appealed to me. I knew I could be an asset in his life.

Tim O'Malley was a tall, distinguished man with thick, blonde hair that he slicked back to show off his high forehead. His bulging green eyes, along with his red-faced complexion, revealed that he had weathered the storm of alcohol. An eligible bachelor of forty-five, he was wealthy and prominent, and we met after my marriage had ended. What could be bad? I thought this was going to be my way "out of prison."

I soon discovered that he was interested exclusively in my body. He used it as a vehicle to fulfill his sexual desires. I allowed myself to be available at his whim—caught in the spider's web, fulfilling his sexual fantasies.

I was gifted in the right places. I had beautiful, full breasts, a small waist, and hips that could make him cry for more. Tim had a fetish about my talking to him while making love. He wanted me to create sexual fantasies. To amuse him, I would make up stories about bizarre pleasures with three or more women, two men and one woman, or two women and one man; whatever I felt would stimulate his sexual imagination. By the time I finished the story, he would usually have fallen asleep, leaving me to put my clothes on and go home.

I allowed myself to stay in this relationship for five years, always vowing never to see him again, until the next phone call. I anguished over it, because it was such a one-dimensional affair. But I had never been one to maintain several love relationships simultaneously and felt more comfortable with a steady partner. I worked two jobs and supported three children, so I didn't have much time for dating. His hectic schedule left little time for socializing, so our brief getaways worked well with our lifestyles.

One day my friend Nancy listened as I told her of my disappointment that Tim didn't seem interested in anything except sex with me.

"Why don't you tell him that the next time he wants to see you, you'll take the money instead of dinner?" she said.

I sat there with my mouth open in shock that Nancy would even suggest such a thing.

She bluntly pointed out that I was his "call girl," so why not get paid for my services?

"You know there is no future for you with Tim and never will be," she said. "You could certainly use the money for the kids, and besides, it's only a fifteen-minute soiree, so make it work to your advantage."

She had planted a seed.

The relationship became more and more demanding. I was beginning to tire of the phone calls and quick dinners for his sexual pleasures. When Tim called late one afternoon to meet for "dinner," I hesitated.

"If you want my body for your sexual satisfaction, pay me in lieu of dinner, and we'll both be happy."

I held my breath for his response.

"I'll be over at eight," he said.

I couldn't believe what I had just said. From that evening on, when he called, which was about once a week, I accepted, knowing that I would be $60 richer. When we were finished in the bedroom, he would go to the bathroom, dress and leave the money on the kitchen counter—three, crisp, twenty-dollar bills. He never handed me the money.

I had confided in my two close friends and told them what I was doing. It became our secret joke. I lived only five minutes from my work, so if Tim called from court and had a long recess, we would meet at my house. The children were in school, and I had an hour for lunch.

"Is it a Campbell's Soup day?" my friends would ask.

"Yes," I would say with a smile, and off I'd go "for lunch."

In time, I moved out of state, and we lost contact.

Several years later, I was back visiting, and as I shopped in the local mall, I saw Tim strutting toward me. He was delighted to see me and suggested that we have a cup of coffee and chat.

"What is happening in your life? I want to hear everything," he said eagerly.

I happily displayed my wedding band.

"A wonderful husband of one year," I said proudly. "What about you? Are you married, living with someone?"

"Yes, I am living with a woman who is president of a prestigious college," he told me. "We have been together for a couple of years," he continued, and then he had the gall to say, "but I want to be with you again. I've missed that wonderful, warm body."

Before he could continue to plead his case, I responded.

"I was your whore once; I won't be that again. I'm married, I love my husband and those marriage vows I took are sacred," I stood up.

"I need to go home," I said politely.

I walked away then and have never seen him again.

I was finally free from my sentence.

PART III
Transition

And Then There Was Change

I learned very quickly that although I worked in a system that appeared structured, abrupt changes in policies and procedures were as much a part of prison life as lockdowns and rules. I liked to think of myself as adaptable to change, but I often felt as though I was riding a roller coaster.

My initial schedule had been set for every Thursday from 3:00 to 4:15 PM. Anne Riter thought that this time slot would work well in the women's daily schedule of classes, meals, prison count and visitations.

Bill C. always greeted me kindly, and we shared a little update about our lives in general. He let the women whose names were on the sign-up sheet into the classroom, which was locked when not in use. I didn't always wear my watch, so Bill C. and I had an understanding that he would knock on the classroom door five minutes before class should end. It was my signal to finish up and get the women out the door so they could walk across the hall for dinner. I structured that hour and fifteen minutes: time for greetings and centering, stretching, and the final relaxation. I felt in control, and the women adapted nicely.

Then, the time started to vary. After eight weeks, Bill C. informed me one day that I needed to end class by 4:00 so that the women could be in the cafeteria by 4:05 for dinner. I could still do a full hour program comfortably with the ten-minute circle of sharing reduced to five. Once again, I settled into a schedule. But one day, about seven weeks after the first change, the women started to show up for class after 3:00 PM.

"What's the hold up?" I asked sharply.

"There was a countdown at 3:00. We needed to be cleared before we could leave our unit," Ariel said. "The rest of the ladies are fuming 'cause they gonna be late."

When Bill C. escorted the rest of the women upstairs, it was already 3:10. I tried to squeeze a little extra time in at the end. Bill C. knocked at the window at 4:00 PM, but I continued the relaxation for a few more minutes, hoping he wouldn't return angry.

The entire prison churned as rumors of impending change circulated constantly. The staff worried about who would lose his or her job and where shift changes and assignments into unfamiliar units would occur.

When I first arrived for class, with the second time change, I sometimes had to go to the unit and ask one of the officers to call downstairs to find a program officer, or to call Anne Riter to find someone to monitor the hallway outside my classroom. On rare occasions, Anne went to the unit herself and brought the women up, leaving a social worker in charge until I finished. This cut our time from the original one hour and fifteen minutes down to forty-five minutes.

Frustrated and discouraged, I cut the exercises to thirty minutes and started with a five-minute introduction in which I asked, "How are you doing today? Close your eyes, and take a few breaths in and out," followed by stretching and ten minutes for relaxation at the end.

Some of the women had questions about the exercises, such as what would benefit low back pain or help release tension during stressful situations, and what exercises they could continue during the week. I tried to address their questions after class. Sometimes they went to the cafeteria late, but it didn't seem to bother them. They sought my advice.

"Standing at the end of the line ain't no big deal for us," Cecily said.

The women loved to share how some of the exercises helped them during the week. I felt it was important to get their feedback, so I stretched time, always nervous that the officer would scold me for not taking them to the cafeteria on time. Each week, I walked away feeling I'd escaped harsh words or a reprimand again. I expressed my frustrations to Anne who assured me she would look into the situation and see what could be worked out.

"For now, continue planning for forty-five minutes," she said.

Sometimes I wanted to quit, but the response from the women was so positive that I just couldn't let them down.

"Don't leave, we need you; we need this class," they often said.

I kept telling myself that the frequent changes of schedule would stop.

However, the problem of finding a program officer got increasingly worse. Bill C. was often called for duty in another section of the jail, and I never knew with whom I would be working until I arrived on the floor. One day the women arrived with only ten minutes left of class. Again, Anne promised she would address the issue with the appropriate higher-ups.

"Be patient," she said. "I apologize." There were internal changes going on which couldn't be discussed at that time.

"Trust me," were Anne's words, and that I did.

A few weeks later, the bombshell hit. Anne told me that both she and Elizabeth Khorn, the director of both the male and female programs, were taking early retirement. Anne had been my anchor. As she prepared to abandon my ship, I experienced panic and wondered if my program would continue.

Who would be my support? I had worked hard to get this Fit and Wellness program implemented. Now what would happen? The entire program had been well received by the inmates and staff for over thirteen months by that point. I had to hold back the tears. I cared about and loved working with these women.

I knew I was teaching them the meaning of commitment, helping them build self-esteem, and encouraging them to stretch far beyond what they believed they were capable of doing. The techniques I taught them would support them when they re-entered the outside world. I read renewed hope in the papers they wrote at the end of each six-week program as they described the positive effects of the class on their lives. We were planting and cultivating seeds together. I didn't want the seeds to stop growing or the opportunity to plant new ones to wither.

Anne promised that she would make sure the program continued.

Two weeks after Anne's decision to leave, she introduced me to a new social worker, Rosemarie, who would be responsible for the women in the recovery unit. Immediately, I felt a warm connection to Rosemarie. She was black and beautiful. Her green eyes sparkled as she spoke, and she smiled frequently. Her clothes were impeccable and the colors were coordinated. Each week her wardrobe made a statement about her artistic inclinations.

"You belong in art school, designing clothes," I wanted to tell her.

◆   ◆   ◆

Rosemarie and Anne made the decision that I should work inside the recovery unit every week and that the class would be compulsory for all inmates. I had arrived as a respected part of the facility's programs! Although I preferred the 10:00 to 11:00 AM hour, it had to be changed for requirements of the unit. We chose 1:00 to 2:00 PM as the new time slot, but Thursday would not work. General Education Diploma and some religious programs were already in place. We chose Monday as my new day.

I was thrilled! The later time would relieve me of contending with the expressway traffic. One o'clock, immediately after lunch, wasn't the best time for exercising, but I was willing to give it a try.

"I'll make it work," I thought.

Rosemarie and Anne decided that after the six-week program in the recovery unit, the women from the general population could sign up for the alternate six weeks in the classroom. They thought that after the stresses of working inside a unit where I would teach twenty-eight women under the watchful eye of one or two officers, I would be ready for a more relaxed atmosphere in a classroom with twelve women.

I wondered if the women would feel free to express their feelings inside a unit, which didn't allow for a small classroom. I hoped the officers would be receptive to my presence.

◆   ◆   ◆

Rosemarie introduced me to Ellen Macki, the new director of the women's programs. Ellen didn't appear welcoming, and I was nervous in her presence. Standing six feet tall, she was a muscular, tanned blonde.

"She looks more suitable for a body-building competition," I thought with envy.

"Give her time, and she'll work with you," my inner voice said. I felt reluctant but gave her a warm handshake.

When Ellen posted a sign-up sheet in the GP unit and only eight signed up, I was disappointed. I usually had to limit registration to twelve, and some inmates had to wait for the next period. Two of the women, Marylyn and Mary, were repeats from the previous classes.

Since my program was pushed back to 1:00–2:00, the inmates seemed tired after lunchtime and focused on relaxing and sleeping. The second week into the program, the women didn't come to me until 1:30.

"We have a new sheriff, and he changed our meal time," Marylyn said.

At the last class, I asked Ellen if I could once again combine both units in the classroom, now that the prison was back at full staff and program officers were in place.

"I'll see what I can do," Ellen promised.

After her conference with the social workers and unit directors, Ellen informed me that it wasn't possible to combine both units. She did not explain her answer, and I knew not to ask any more questions. I had to work with the existing system if I wanted to continue.

Rosemarie, the social worker in the recovery unit, had transferred to the men's unit, and I felt lost without those around me in power who believed in what I was doing. My anchor, Anne Riter, had been uprooted, and now Rosemarie was also abandoning my ship.

"It's much easier working with the men," Rosemarie explained. "I needed a change after five years in the women's unit."

I had heard several female officers say they preferred working in the men's units. I wondered why, but I never took the opportunity to explore this issue further.

Maci Hubbs, Rosemarie's replacement, was soon scheduled to run twelve-step programs in the recovery unit from 1:00 to 2:00.

"You need to change your schedule," Ellen informed me.

Exasperated, I bit my tongue and waited to hear where I could fit into the system.

Sitting at her desk checking schedules on her calendar, Ellen looked up at me.

"Why not do your class from 10:00 to 11:00?" she suggested. At last, she was working with me. That was exactly the time slot I had wanted when I'd first started. The women would be more attentive, I would have very little traffic to contend with, and the rest of the day left me with down time.

Perfect! I thought.

Last Class Before Going Inside the Recovery Unit

What a day! The inmates were wildly vocal!

After working with these women for months, we had experienced yet another schedule change that intensified the upset they felt about the recent layoffs of staff. They wondered where they fit into this new prison schedule. They were scared.

The women knew I would be teaching only inside the recovery unit due to the recent loss of personnel and programs. The course would be ongoing and mandatory for everyone. Women from different units would no longer be allowed to mingle, so the GP population couldn't participate, much as they wanted to continue.

I heard "this sucks" several times. "I'm going to write a letter to the sheriff," Bethany said.

They were disgusted with this change that impacted their lives.

Cecily wanted to talk, so I let her have the floor. She explained that it would be impossible for me to teach in their unit (the GP), because there are usually fifty to sixty women. They are all ages and not respectful of the privacy of others.

"Last Sunday, a Catholic priest and his assistant came to say Mass in the unit because the chapel was closed," she said. "The entire time he was saying Mass, over half of the unit was screaming, laughing, and jumping all over the place."

"What were the officers doing?" I asked. "Didn't they try to control the situation?"

"They were yelling and laughing along with the inmates," she replied. "If you hug, kiss, fuck, suck, and cuss, you are in! Everyone else is fair game for anything that happens in the unit." Cecily was visibly angry.

I felt my throat tighten after hearing that amazing description of what life was really like in the prison, but I got the picture and couldn't wait to tell someone what I had just heard. I always wondered about the prison life I didn't see.

I applauded Cecily for her direct honesty.

"Thank you for sharing that information," I said.

So, if you didn't adhere to the in-crowd rules, you would be tormented by the inmate leaders. Every unit had leaders and followers. I imagined that the followers were in a precarious position and would be called upon to perform in a variety of unpleasant ways.

The GP ladies wanted me to ask Ellen Macki if I could do a six-week program in the classroom. I sensed they were feeling abandoned, and I promised I would speak to Ellen about it.

Some women began to talk openly about the officers. Twanda led the group.

"The males are much easier to work with than the females. Them females are always yelling, and most of them are in constant hormonal rage. You don't have periods thirty days a month," she said.

The rest of the group laughed and shook their heads in agreement. Nancy named a few officers who were civil to them.

"Everett, Smith and Lopez are our favorites," she said, and the group agreed.

"The rest," they said, "enjoy barking orders."

I was grateful I didn't encounter the wrath of the officers.

I dialed my husband's cell phone as soon as I got to the car. I needed to process all I had heard in class. This was the first time they had been so open in front of me, and I loved being part of their lives. While fighting the expressway dinner traffic, I rambled on about the terms they used and how openly they had behaved. Ed listened politely.

"That's nice," he said when I finished.

"Did you hear what I said?" I shouted.

He hesitated. "I have Jeff with me, and I'm taking him to the airport. We'll talk tonight," he said in a monotone.

I got the message, but I wanted to talk then.

I felt frustrated driving home. Having made a strong connection with these women, I wanted to share my experience at that very moment.

"This sucked," as Cecily would have said.

◆　　◆　　◆

By the eighth graduation, problems I'd previously encountered seemed to occur less often. It was hard to believe that I'd guided eight groups through to completion. I had adjusted to the system's structure.

Bethany had asked me the previous week to write the name Susan Temple instead of Bethany Rhines on her certificate. When she arrived in class, as I was talking to Anne Riter, Bethany asked Anne if she could change the name on the certificate. Anne refused, because Bethany Rhines was the name on her prison records.

"But I am going to court next week to have my name changed," Bethany pleaded.

Anne answered rather loudly, "You came in as Bethany Rhines, and that's the way you'll go out. The next time you come in, you can use your new name if it's legal."

I wanted to ask Bethany why she intended to change her name, but the opportunity didn't present itself, and I felt sad about Anne's quick assumption that Bethany would be back.

Afterwards, walking down the hallway in serious thought, I bumped into Mimie Rump, one of the ladies I had met in my second graduating class, and who I'd last seen on parole day, outside the prison entrance. Startled, our eyes met. We remained silent, waiting to see who was going to speak first. She looked at the floor.

"I'm only here for a parole violation. It's just for a couple of weeks," she said softly.

"But you are back in jail, regardless of the reason," I wanted to say.

I remembered the sweetness of her voice, her smile as she entered the classroom each week, so excited about the program. She had seemed accepting of everything I taught, absorbing my every word like a sponge. She had tried all the postures with no complaints, even though some of the forward and back bends were difficult for her.

Mimie's body was twenty pounds heavier than when she first came in to prison. She had never experienced physical exercise except in the high school gym. Mimie, who had been in the recovery unit when she participated in her first class, now wore the GP brown uniform. I guessed her violation wasn't alcohol or drugs.

"I am going to sign up for your next session," she said, smiling.

A quick handshake, and down the hall she disappeared. I felt sad about seeing her back in jail. What had she really learned? As I waited for the elevator, I wondered how many more I would encounter coming back through the revolving door.

The next week, I would satisfy my curiosity about what went on behind the closed doors of a special unit.

Inside the Recovery Unit

I approached the unit door slowly and pressed my face against the window for a glimpse of my new classroom. I saw the wooden doors of the cells with narrow, vertical windows strategically placed within direct view of two officers, who stood with their backs to the main door and their bodies in full view of the inmates. The officers congregated behind a circular desk laden with a phone and colored buttons on a switchboard that they could press for emergency or medical help and could use to open and close the main door to the unit.

This is like visiting an animal shelter, I thought as I glanced at the women's cell doors.

I remembered those doggies barking, waiting to be given freedom.

"Pick me, I'll be good." I remembered their voices from the many times I had visited the shelter with my grandchildren. I peeked around the room, looking into the eyes of the women who waited to be released for the program. Some smiled, and others waved. Off to the right, I saw Cecily. Her nose and forehead were pressed so tightly against the window of her room that I could see the heat coming off her body.

"Get me out of here!" all the eyes seemed to beg.

I pressed the outside buzzer; an officer turned, perplexed. I held up my volunteer badge and was buzzed in.

"Why is it so quiet?" I asked.

"There's been a shakedown. All the women are in their cells until the unit has been cleared," the female officer at the front desk explained.

The recovery unit of the prison housed eighteen to forty women who were recovering from dependency on alcohol, drugs, gambling, or other addictions. The women were searched for illegal items during intermittent shakedowns. Officers thoroughly examined inmates' rooms for contraband such as needles, pipes, money, towels, extra bed linens or blankets. Each woman had to remove her clothes while a female officer inspected the inmate's entire body, including private parts. They were asked to lift their arms, open their mouths and bend forward so that their hips were raised and their rectums and vaginas were in full view. Women would sometimes conceal illegal possessions in those areas, hoping to escape detection.

On my extreme right as I entered the unit, ten black leather chairs were clustered together for those who wanted to watch television. A 28" TV was mounted to a wall unit about six feet from the floor—higher than the tallest woman. The inmates could watch television at designated times. There was no cable service.

At the far end of the space stood a washing machine and dryer. I noticed that they were not coin operated. I had thought that the women were responsible for their personal laundry and obligated to pay for this convenience.

Next to these appliances was a bathroom with toilets and sinks. There were three separate shower stalls nearby. I was amazed at the privacy the inmates received for showering; it seemed such a contrast to the random strip searches. The shower rooms had the same wooden doors and long, narrow windows as the women's cells.

Up against the cement wall next to the main door were five wall phones in bright blue with black receivers. The inmates had to call collect. Certain times were designated for this privilege. It was stressful when eight or nine women all needed to use the phone at the same time. I heard more "get the fuck off the phone," and "you motor mouth, your time is up," than "please," or "I'd appreciate ..."

Although the outward appearance was orderly, daily living under these conditions was stressful. When forty women lived together twenty-four hours a day, conflict frequently broke out as they coped with pregnancies, menstrual cycles, drug detox, boredom, and frustration. Women directly involved in trouble ended up in "the hole" in solitary confinement, the length of which was determined by the degree of violence of the transgression.

When I began teaching in the unit, there were thirty-eight women, which was very near the facility's capacity of forty. This unit was generally full. As women left on parole, more moved in to take their places.

For some inmates it was a safe haven—meals three times a day, bed, clothing, showers and someone to watch over them. The recovery unit offered protection and rest from the rugged outside environments that brought women to prison. Some of the women worked the street and slept in alleyways near their territories. In prison, there was warmth, food and protection and no pimp to beat you up for not turning tricks.

This reminded me of when I worked in the hospital. Occasionally some people who lived on the streets and saw winter approaching would deliberately allow themselves to be hit by cars, hoping for just enough injuries to be in the hospital for a few months until signs of spring approached.

◆   ◆   ◆

Sue Johnson, a short-haired, blonde officer, was on duty that day. Her gabardine trousers fit perfectly, highlighting her flat stomach and small hips, and her short-sleeved shirt revealed strong arms. She spoke about socializing with the other officers; she had her eye on one of the eligible bachelors and wondered if she could fit into his life. She amused me with anecdotes about a recent party a lot of the officers had attended.

However, I soon learned that Sue was a no-nonsense officer on the job. If the women were the least bit disrespectful in words or actions, she immediately sent them back to their cells. Twenty to forty women inside a small unit could present a challenge when doing exercise, meditation and relaxation, and Sue helped me by speaking out when some of the inmates talked or snickered. I gave her permission to correct the women during my class and, if necessary, send them back to their cells. In that way, I welcomed her authority.

Sue's work partner had skin the color of milk chocolate, smooth and creamy, and bright, big brown eyes. Her eyelids looked like window shades that had been opened wide. Her lips were thick and luscious with just a faint trace of lipstick. Her badge, pinned on the right pocket of her shirt, identified her as Savannah Courte. Savannah's trousers fit more like a sarong, accenting her round hips. She was showing in front—a small bulge near her zipper. I sensed she must have had a baby or two and not lost all the weight gained during pregnancy.

An officer's formal uniform consisted of a starched blue shirt, long or short-sleeved, with a navy and yellow badge bearing the name of the prison on the left sleeve. The buttons on Savannah's shirt were starting to pop holes. Her navy tie had a clip with the prison insignia. A pin in the shape of a star, also with the prison insignia, decorated her shirt collar. Savannah's eyes followed me, and I knew she was curious about the program. She asked no questions during the class; she simply observed.

Each inmate received one set of sheets, one blanket, one towel, and one wash cloth. There were no pillows. They slept on a soft, thin cot, bunk-bed style, usually two women to a room. If there was an overload of inmates, some were given a third roommate. The quarters then became very crowded. Locks on the outside of these rooms confined the women if riots or chaos erupted.

Outside their rooms was a large space in the shape of an L, with three tables. Each table had four seats attached to it and was a place where the women could do their paperwork for court and parole hearings, write letters home and read.

The common area was adorned with drawings from the inmates' children. Some were pages ripped from a coloring book; others were scrawled on plain sheets of paper for "Mommy." Many displayed vivid colors—bright reds and blues. Some had the child's name underneath; others read, "I love you."

These youthful illustrations on the concrete walls camouflaged the coldness of the prison environment. The majority of women in the prison had children, mostly under the age of ten. Their families usually consisted of mother, grandmother and children—adult males were rarely in the picture. Most inmates were not married. All shared the same sentiment: "I miss my kids so much."

For some families who visited a loved one here, jail was perceived as a safe place, where someone they cared for could heal. In prison, their loved one could not bring harm to herself or others. For a period of time, families rest, knowing where their loved ones are. For a while there is no tension or pressure. Arguments and police at the door are absent.

"It's a relief for my family," said Cecily. "They's happy and sad I'm in here."

Monthly Canteen

I felt proud of my eighteen months of teaching. I had just finished another six weeks with the GP women and was back in the recovery unit for my fourth time. Ellen introduced me to a new officer, Elise Natum, who had just returned from maternity leave. She was a bubbly woman, and I liked her immediately.

"Please put any woman in her cell if snickering, rudeness or inattention erupts," I said, smiling.

Elise nodded approvingly.

"You also have my permission to tell them to exit," she said.

This time I had a small group—sixteen—compared with previous groups of twenty-eight or more. The reason for the low count was that most of the rest of the women had to attend preparation classes for the GED. Some lingered in the unit, watching us until Elise told them to leave. Reba and Traci had often said that they felt my program was more important than a GED. They wrote a letter to their social worker requesting an exemption from the GED classes, but to no avail.

I enjoyed working with a smaller group; it gave me more control, and I had time to instruct those who were having difficulty with specific postures. As I scanned the room, I saw some familiar faces but noticed the absence of my spike-haired gal, Victoria. Before I had an opportunity to ask about her, Cecily informed me that Victoria was in lockdown for two days, having assaulted her roommate, torn her books, and eaten all her candy.

"How are things going?" Maci, the new social worker, asked me after class.

"I like working with the women in recovery but find it better teaching in the classroom. In the unit, some women take bathroom breaks, and there are always people coming in and out," I answered.

"There are no scheduled programs in the classroom this time of day. Tell Ellen you spoke with me, and I gave my thumbs up for you to use it instead," Maci said without hesitation.

I hurried into Ellen's office, presented her with the information and held my breath for approval.

She checked her calendar closely, looking over the daily schedule, and said, "The only way you can use the classroom is to change your hour back to one o'clock. The GED studies are compulsory for both units in the morning and that is the only classroom available. It's your call."

Ugh, I thought. That would be right after lunch and back to the old schedule, but I really wanted the privacy and control, so I accepted the classroom and the old time slot. Ellen emphatically reminded me that the women from the different units must remain separate. I wondered why; we had mixed them earlier. But I knew not to push for answers. I left with mixed feelings, hoping I'd made the right decision.

◆   ◆   ◆

When I arrived for my last class in the unit, the women were enjoying social time, drinking coffee and eating cookies. Some watched "The View" on television, and two were on the phone.

"Time for Fit and Wellness," Elise shouted. "Let's get moving!" she called in an even more ear-shattering tone.

A couple of the women quickly moved the tables out of the way so we could sit on the floor in a circle.

As we began, one of the lieutenants came in for a routine inspection, then stopped and watched our group stretching.

"What the hell is that all about?" he asked Officer Natum, pointing to us.

She whispered in his ear, then he shook his head and left.

I wondered what portrayal he would present to others about this unit's activities.

As usual, I asked the ladies to pick their favorite exercises and lead the group in doing a specific posture during the last week of the program. Maria raised her hand to be first. She leapt up, and in half-Spanish, half-English, she led the group in a perfect tree pose.

Rosa and Cecily demonstrated partner yoga, sitting on the floor, pressing feet to feet and stretching arms forward and backward, releasing tension in the back. They did several variations of these stretches on the floor, which everyone loved.

I saw Elise stretching while at her station. I was convinced the officers needed a program like mine. Everyone would benefit, both the staff and inmates, if the officers could release some of their tension, too.

Just as we were getting ready for relaxation, the doors swung open, and in stomped two men with big, yellow laundry carts. They paused at the officer's station, stared at me and then proceeded to the tables at the far end of the unit, taking out big, brown paper bags and shouting, "Rivers, Jones."

The two women quickly got up, took their bags and hurried to their rooms.

"Who are these men?" I whispered to the group.

"The guys from the canteen. They deliver our personal stuff: shampoo, toothpaste, candy, cookies, whatever else we need," Rosa answered. "If we don't pick up our orders, we have to wait another month," Rosa whispered, afraid of being heard.

I found out later that the women paid for those articles with cash earned there, a dollar a day, or money brought in by the family that was put into a personal account. I remembered seeing a newly installed ATM machine in the lobby, probably for the convenience of the families.

As Maria, a tiny grandmother of twelve, hurried to her room with her filled bag, my gaze followed her into her cell. I watched her pile hard candy and candy bars so high on her cot, I thought they would topple. Mountainous peaks, some wide and others pointed. *Oh my God!* I thought. I could not imagine one person eating all that candy. Was she doing favors for her friends in return for candy? How did she ever accumulate such a supply? Was this a substitute for her drug addiction?

I felt sad.

After ten minutes, the canteen men left. I took the women into a deep relaxation, one that I desperately needed after all those interruptions.

Ellen Macki came in as we ended class and informed the women that I would be back in six weeks, but in the classroom. They all cheered and clapped, as happy as I was about the change. Ellen read their six-week papers and was pleased to see that the program had been so well received.

As we left the unit, I told Ellen about the interruptions and distractions from the canteen men.

"I understand the need for a classroom," she said. "The sign-up sheet will be hung in the GP unit for your next six weeks. No more teaching inside the unit."

I left prison frazzled by the disruptions, noises and impending changes. Would I ever settle into one place and one time?

I think I already knew the answer to that question.

Holiday in the
Recovery Unit

As I drove to the prison, I remembered that it was the Veteran's Day holiday and wondered if there would be any changes in visiting privileges and programs.

Only three officers congregated outside the building. Inside, I was stiffly questioned about what I carried and had to go back to the front desk to show the authorization paper containing the name of the CD, my Tibetan bells and even my pen and glasses.

"Where is everyone?" I asked a new officer at the front desk.

"Social services are closed, and we're always short-staffed on holidays," he answered. "That's why I hate to work holidays. I'm doing my job and those of six other people."

He continued grumbling under his breath.

Months before, I had been cleared to bring a meditation book rather than having to rely on memory, thanks to Anne's approval, and carried with me a wonderful meditation for connecting with the heart. The previous week, I had done a meditation focusing on communicating and dealing with relationships in a peaceful manner. Rosemarie, the social worker in the recovery unit, had offered a thumbs up. "I need to do more of this quiet time," she said in an enthusiastic voice.

Being a morning person, I loved my new 10 to 11 AM class time. The staff seemed more relaxed, and my entrance and exit felt less stressful. The officers at the front desk usually greeted me pleasantly and sent me through security and up to the unit with a wave.

Today on the holiday, though, I felt nervous, wondering which officers would be on duty in the unit. I felt fairly comfortable with the regular ones, but who knew what a holiday would bring?

An officer always watched me closely. I felt I needed to be cautious when asking the women questions about their daily lives. It wasn't forbidden, but I didn't want the officers to get the impression I was more interested in their personal lives than in the program I presented.

"How was your week?" I asked. "Who has been practicing these exercises? How about those on a diet?"

I kept it simple. I wanted to be accepted by following the rules, making a good impression.

I experienced more distractions inside the unit than just the canteen men. Occasionally, a nurse would come in to give an inmate medication or to take blood. Some women were diabetic and their insulin levels had to be checked. Often, names were called out while we were doing a meditation. Sometimes, a new officer dropped off mail, often stopping to watch for a few minutes, then smiled and left. I hoped good words filtered through the other units.

This Veteran's Day, the women were scattered in all directions. Books were out on some of the tables, and several groups congregated and chatted in different parts of the open area. I saw more activity than I usually encountered. As I signed in, I felt disappointed to learn from Sue that Rosemarie was off for the holiday.

Rosemarie's presence always brought structure, and I would miss her when she transferred to the men's unit. Since the CD player was locked in her office, there would be no soft music to relax the women. In my previous classes, as soon as I turned on the CD player and music filled the room, they began to quiet down.

I asked the women to put away their books, move the tables to the back of the room, and clear the space for exercising. I reluctantly rang the bells for silence. I asked if there were new people, and three women raised their hands. I explained the program and the rules and asked if they had any questions.

"I have my period and can't do these exercises," said Jenna.

"How do you know if you haven't tried?" I asked.

She looked for the others to agree with her, but no one responded. The other two new women, Kelley and Andi, waved their hands, but they only had comments, no questions.

I was drawn to Andi's pink hair, which was bound in tight braids. It was the brightest color pink I'd ever seen. She turned her head in all directions and constantly pulled at her braids, a nervous mannerism. I wasn't sure she followed instructions well. She danced to a different drummer. Andi seemed agitated, and that made me nervous. I reminded myself that this was a recovery unit. Andi might have been coming off heroin or cocaine. It was frustrating to work with these women without knowing their backgrounds. I learned to go with my gut feelings since the officers didn't offer any information. I paid attention to what I heard the inmates say and relied on my inner voice.

When I had them seated in a circle, one of the women asked about the bells.

"They are Tibetan bells used by monks to initiate meditation, but they are more commonly used for calling one forth into the here and now," I answered.

They asked me about the sound "om"—what it meant and why people chanted it. I explained that "om" was traditionally used as a meditative sound to still the mind, invoke inner peace and expand awareness. It originated in the east but had become a universal symbol. I was impressed by their attention.

"I miss the soft music today. I guess it relaxes me," Kelley said.

"Yes, it's one of the ways to relax the body and mind to focus on the postures we're doing. It allows us to connect at a deeper level with our bodies."

So, we talked a little about vibration, music and sound. Jenna said that she liked to listen to country and western music. It took her mind off being in jail. Music by Kenny Rogers was her favorite. I saw Tina make a face when Jenna mentioned country and western. I heard a few snickers. This annoyed me and the rest of the group.

"If you don't want to be in this class, go to your cells or refrain from snide comments," I told Marylyn and Mary, who sat in the back. That was a good time to reinforce the importance of their commitment to the program.

"If you aren't committed, go to your cell," I repeated again in a firm tone. In that moment, "cell" seemed the appropriate word. They made faces but stopped talking.

"I want to participate, earn my good time, and receive my certificate." I was glad to hear Sue speak up.

"I need all the good time I can grab to get out of this hell hole," Andi said, nervously nodding her head.

I was beginning to get dizzy watching her movements.

"I hear ya," someone said, and others nodded.

I felt on edge during class; picking up their erratic energy, I had difficulty concentrating myself. As I demonstrated the standing stretches, I struggled for a flow of postures, but the flow didn't happen until it was time to do the heart meditation. I instructed them to lie comfortably on the floor, close their eyes and begin to relax by taking a few deep inhalations and slow exhalations.

One of the women, Tina, abruptly left the unit as I gave the breathing instructions. I thought she had a medical appointment, but a few minutes later, she came back with a big grin on her face. She carried a CD player, quietly plugged it in and extended her hand for the CD. She pressed the play button, and the soft sounds of the flute began.

I felt the energy shift in the group. The static had turned to a wave of calm. I felt grateful to Tina for bringing peace to the group, although it was such a mystery that she knew where to find the CD player. I felt confused at how she so easily entered and exited the unit.

Throughout the heart meditation, we experienced complete silence; only the music in the background could be heard.

The officer rolled her eyes as if to say, "I can't believe this silence." When I finished the meditation, I asked the group to share their experiences.

Tina raised her hand. "I asked my sister for forgiveness. I spent a night with her boyfriend and got pregnant. She ain't spoke to me since." Her eyes filled with tears.

"Maybe you should write your sister an apology letter," I suggested.

Hesitantly, Marcy raised her hand. "I asked that the dove in the meditation bring me to my children."

Belinda, young and quiet, said that she told her dove all she wanted was food, food, and more food. Then, she laughed to cover herself. I didn't want to let her off easily.

"You should look at that metaphor. The food represents your need to be loved and nurtured, but using food hasn't provided you with that nourishment," I said. "What do you think could give you love?"

The women nodded vigorously, appearing to understand the metaphor. "I told you, Belinda, to stop stuffing your face and start loving your body," shouted Tina.

Belinda hung her head and laughed.

Did she hear the message? I wondered.

I had never been so grateful for a class to end. "What was their problem today? They acted like caged animals," I asked Sue Johnson.

"They haven't had any supervision since Friday. With Rosemarie off, they have been left to their own devices," Sue replied.

They really needed structured programs. Most were not able to initiate positive activities for themselves.

I talked to Cecily, who had stayed out of the hole for the past couple of weeks and was trying harder than ever to keep her mouth shut and her hands to herself. This was her second time in prison.

"Never again," she said.

I warned her to go slow, take one day at a time. I complimented her on being active in my class.

She hung her head shyly, and I wondered if she ever received compliments from anyone else.

I left her with a suggestion. "When things start to get out of control, stop, take a breath in, hold it for the count of four and then slowly let it out, and you'll begin to feel more in control and stay out of trouble."

She nodded approvingly and gave me a big hug. She was up for parole at the end of the month and was focused on getting out.

Before we ended the class, I asked how many had children. Almost all raised their hands.

"Is there anyone who doesn't have children?" I asked, smiling. Only three responded.

As I left the room, Rhonda, who usually sat in the back, approached me.

"I want to thank you for volunteering your services," she said and extended her hand for a shake of friendship.

"Here is my gift for today!" I thought. "Hang in there. They do appreciate you," my inner voice said.

I couldn't help thinking about the women's children, though; were they in foster care? Were they living with relatives? Were they left to their own devices wherever they were living? Those children would shape our future, and I wondered what messages were shaping their lives and chances of survival.

I saw two officers chatting in the cafeteria, waiting for their shift to start.

"Will one of you get the elevator for me?"

Ann, who had been in the unit with me twice, nodded and jumped up to help. From behind the doorway, PJ, a young woman from the GP unit whom I knew from a previous class, appeared. Standing with a scrub bucket and mop in hand, ready to scrub the hall floor, she stopped and greeted me with an affectionate hello.

"When are you coming back to our unit?" she asked enthusiastically.

I explained that I had two more weeks with the recovery group. Then I would start a six-week program for the general population.

She smiled and shared that she gave her mother the certificate she received for completion of my program. "My mama has it hanging up in the living room for everyone to see," PJ said, with great pride. "This was my first certificate, and I hope I can earn more while I'm in here to make my mama proud."

As I listened to her describe her feelings of accomplishment, I wanted to cry. I wondered if she realized how powerful her words felt to me. That inner voice again said, "Hang in there."

After I left PJ, I stopped off at Anne Riter's office to go over some last-minute details about my program. Anne would leave the following week to begin early retirement after fifteen years of service at this facility. I would truly miss her support and all the great work she had done implementing programs for the ladies. She told me that the women had spoken highly about the program and hoped that it would continue when she left. She assured them that it would. She reminded them that the few programs available were mostly provided by volunteers.

"Appreciate the time and effort they put into being here," Anne told the women. She said that the new women's prison was scheduled to open in two months. The staff hoped that more social workers and officers would be hired and that there would be more programs like mine implemented.

I left that day with mixed feelings. PJ and Rhonda were my gifts, but I felt so disconnected from my body that I couldn't wait to have a session with my therapist.

Therapy

I had felt frazzled since Monday and was happy to be driving to my appointment with Andrew Ford, my therapist of fourteen years. In the past two days, I had managed to squeeze in a yoga class, in which I was a participant instead of the teacher. After a one-and-a-half-hour workout, I had begun to feel more centered. Monday's class had really jolted my psyche.

I walked up Andrew's newly painted gray steps, holding the wrought-iron railing for support, realizing my physical tiredness. I pressed the buzzer and heard his steps coming to greet me. My thoughts dwelled on the holiday events in prison, and I wondered how we would approach my feelings and reactions to the women and what kind of learning experience this would be for me.

Andrew, who was not a traditional therapist in shirt and tie, wore khakis and a t-shirt, which were pieces of his standard wardrobe. His curly gray and white locks were neatly captured in a ponytail. His piercing green eyes, above a goatee and mustache, observed me carefully. Andrew spoke in a soft, soothing tone, and I immediately felt comforted.

As we walked up the stairs, exchanging pleasantries, I saw a familiar Indian blanket of crimson and gold draped over his blue tweed couch, where we had held many healing sessions previously. My nose picked up the scent of sage recently burned, and my body began to relax.

As soon as I was seated, I poured out my recent experiences at the prison and asked how to handle the frazzled feeling if it came up again. I was at a loss in my understanding of what value the prison classes held for me lately. What could I learn from the women? What were they here to show me?

Andrew's favorite instruction, "close your eyes," was not always mine, but that day I knew the value of journey time and felt eager to see what images, words and guides would appear for me. As my eyes gently closed, Andrew asked me to breathe in the sky and connect with the earth. As I was breathing and relaxing, breathing and relaxing, Andrew asked me to call upon a guide or animal to appear and lead me to the lesson.

I visualized a stag with beautiful antlers standing tall and straight. He looked regal. The deer stepped aside quickly as a cougar rushed past, then resumed his position, standing tall and strong.

"What does the deer have to show you?" Andrew asked.

It reminded me of a beautiful mountain, I told Andrew, solid and tall, containing all seasons. As I began to climb, returning to the journey again, I encountered snow and cold winds. Continuing on, I struggled against ice mixed with snow but eventually found a patch of green grass and some bushes that clung to the mountainside. I stopped for a short rest, breathing in the smells of spring, then traveled to the summit. I slipped occasionally, but there was always a branch or bush to hold onto as I left behind the snow, ice, wind and rain. Finally, I could see the top with great clarity. I felt good about this ascent and the mountain I had chosen to climb.

"Thank the deer for being with you on this journey," Andrew said. "Now gently open your eyes."

I felt surprisingly energized.

"What does this mean to you?" Andrew asked.

"I feel I have the power to control the class and the women," I replied. "If I need to, I can use my authority over the ones who are loud and boisterous and ask the officer to have them removed from class. That would mean no attendance credit for the day and no time off their sentence. Upon completion of my class, they get seven days off their sentence. Since there are not a lot of programs in place, they have an incentive to behave well. It's their choice."

I felt it was important to share the intimacy of my emotional connection with the women I taught. This was my mountain—tall, powerful and treacherous, but rewarding.

Graduation

At some point, Anne thought it would be a good idea to present my students with their Fit and Wellness certificates at the formal graduation for all the women who were receiving their GEDs and other certificates.

"This ceremony makes the women feel special in front of their fellow inmates. They walk up to the stage when their names are called, and this gives them a sense of accomplishment and pride," Anne explained.

I was elated at the thought of being there and participating in their graduation. I was also curious and wondered if I would get to see some of my previous students.

As soon as I walked into the lobby, I saw Luvell dressed in a beige suit with matching pumps. She looked like she might have when she used to teach her college students. I could picture her in front of a class, captivating the students.

"Are you here for graduation?" I asked hesitantly.

"I'm in a halfway house and am back to receive my certificates and do some singing," she said, clearly excited. "Have you seen Sui?"

"No, why would I?" I asked. Not only was it against the rules to socialize with the inmates outside of jail, but I had no intention of doing so. This was my work, not my private life.

Luvell abruptly turned to the officer at the desk, handed her papers to him and went through the detector without answering my question. She sure was in a hurry to go upstairs. I wondered if she intended to stop by the recovery unit and greet her friends.

Anne appeared and gestured for me to follow her. We entered a large room with shiny hardwood floors where about a hundred folding chairs were set up in rows. The lack of windows didn't bother me—it felt like a school auditorium, which seemed appropriate for the event at hand. It reminded me of when I was in Catholic high school, and we periodically had gatherings, including graduation, in the gym.

Two female officers stood at attention by the door, their arms behind their backs. I wondered if I was about to be frisked. I remembered the way nuns stood at the classroom doors to quell any fighting or roughhousing that might erupt. I hadn't wanted my parents to receive a phone call or note regarding my unruly behavior.

Anne stopped to talk to the officers, and I proceeded, untouched, into the room. A cluster of women in business attire surrounded a table where copies of the program were available. I recognized some social workers among them and began to feel more comfortable. I picked up a program and sat down to read it. The program, printed in bright purple and white, looked as if some of the inmates had designed it on the computers in the library.

The inmates entered and marched in single file to their seats. I was surprised to see them in stylish hairdos, like braids and French twists. Not one uniform looked wrinkled; shoes were clean and tied. The women sat at attention, and I sensed pride emanating from them. They were treating this graduation as if it were as significant as graduation ceremonies outside the prison walls.

A small, makeshift stage with six chairs and a podium with a microphone were assembled in front of the rows of chairs. Huge, multi-colored, crepe-paper flowers in jars flanked either side of the stage.

I recognized Gladys from the GP unit and wondered if her husband was still incarcerated. I saw all my women from the most recent class and some from months ago. Some smiled and nodded in recognition, and Lily gave me a thumbs-up, "glad you're here," sign.

I hoped I wouldn't have to say anything or present their certificates. I never did well on presentations or delivering impromptu speeches.

The women were hushed, staring intently at the officials as they entered the auditorium. The sheriff and his assistant led the way, followed by Director of Social Services William Bradley, Anne Riter and Rosemarie, who was Mistress of Ceremonies. This was Rosemarie's last official duty before going into the men's unit. It was nice to see her smiling face.

Rosemarie asked the Reverend Ms. Spence to come up and say a few words. I remembered my high school principal, Father Parkins, would stand up with a welcome and then offer a few short prayers, if we were lucky. On occasion we said the rosary, which was boring to a lot of us, and instead we passed notes about boys, homework and whatever else we could write about to entertain ourselves while others were praying.

The Reverend Ms. Spence was a dark-skinned, ultra-thin woman with short hair that looked de-frizzed. She wore wire-rimmed glasses and a navy gabardine suit. She shouted, "Are you saved? Are you ready to give up prison life and come clean?"

I was startled, but the inmates shouted back, "YES!"

"Have you given up your evil ways?" the reverend continued.

"YES!" the women answered in unison. "Aaaaa-men!"

I felt I had wandered into a revival meeting. The Reverend continued to exhort her audience with quotes from the Bible, to which the women answered, "Amen!"

I felt uncomfortable and hoped the Reverend would soon finish, Amen.

This type of revival gathering was foreign to me, since I had been forbidden to watch any type of prayer gathering on television as a youngster. It was a sin, I was told, and I believed what I was told. That day, although I no longer believed in that kind of sin, I felt uneasy.

Anne Riter then gave the opening speech. Near the end, she said goodbye and thanked everyone—the teachers and the inmates—involved in the programs. She choked up, and so did I. The audience gave her a standing ovation.

Luvell stepped up to the podium. She was beaming as she explained "Sisters with Sound," a program she had developed while in prison. She talked about how some women from the recovery unit loved to sing. Luvell had held practice weekly, and the singing group performed at holidays and special ceremonies for all the units. Thirteen women came to the front, and Luvell then led them in four gospel songs. The audience sat in silence, taking in the healing tones from their voices. They sang from their souls.

Maria belted out beautiful melodies from *West Side Story* in Spanish. She opted to stand on the floor, directly facing the inmates. Petite grandmother though she was, Maria had a voice that could be heard throughout the room with no need for a microphone. As she sang, I remembered her excitement about going home in a few weeks to see her kids and grandkids. She had babysat for some of them while her daughters worked. Maria had been in the recovery unit for the past eighteen months, and I had no idea why she had been incarcerated.

Luvell came on the stage again, giving a pep talk about herself, her many degrees and accomplishments, and the lessons she learned during her incarceration. I listened and watched her, wondering how a multi-talented woman like Luvell could continually come back to prison. She sang "Bridge over Troubled Waters," and I was amazed at the strength in her voice. I imagined her singing in concert as an Aretha Franklin, bringing soul music back to the hit parade. Again, I wondered why Luvell continued to use the revolving door.

The sheriff, deputy and other officials all took turns at the microphone next. My attention wandered until the sheriff talked about the programs and mentioned mine. It had taken me a long time to get that program into the prison, and it was good to be recognized.

Watching the women go up to receive their certificates, I felt my throat tighten more than once. They were all smiles, because they'd achieved something, and their achievement was being recognized. Some were enjoying recognition for the first time in their lives.

My high school graduation diploma had been just a stepping stone for me, a piece of paper that allowed me to further my education. I was happy to be out of that particular prison, in which boys trooped up one set of stairs and the girls skipped up another. I smiled, remembering that on our last day of school, several of my friends and I ran up and down the boys' stairs. We broke the rules.

In prison, you pay for the rules you break.

The Reunion

I had a month of rest and relaxation after my last session in the recovery unit, longer than usual. I had previous commitments that couldn't be changed, and there was a holiday in April, Patriot's Day. Ellen Macki decided it would be best to start the next session around the first of May.

Educational programs that started at the beginning of the month made it easier to keep attendance records. If the women attended a certain number of programs per month, they earned 7.5 hours of time off their sentence.

I had not been with the women from the general population for three months when I started the new six-week program with them. I was looking forward to working with the GP women, because I would be teaching them in the greater privacy of the classroom. It was easier to create a more relaxed atmosphere in which the women could open up about their lives in prison and outside. They spoke freely about their home lives, families and sometimes their reasons for incarceration. They expressed their feelings when we shared after meditation; some even shed tears as they described their journeys.

It felt good, after a month away, to walk into the lobby and approach the front desk, handing the officer my license and getting my special visitor's pass to clip on the front of my sweater. I was relieved to see the usual detector and familiar officers at the desk. They nodded their recognition with smiles and friendly "hellos." I was excited to see who had signed up for my program. I always enjoyed meeting new people who would bring fresh experiences into the class. These women would share their stories, I hoped.

I stopped at Ellen's office to get my sign-up sheet and CD player and to hang my jacket on a hook in her office. I exchanged pleasantries with her secretary, Joni Sweet, who was always interested in the latest CD flute music I brought. Sometimes after class, I would leave the CD with her for the week.

Ellen escorted me to the eleventh floor. We stopped in the cafeteria to speak with Officer Menendez, an older Hispanic woman, who was one of the few well-loved and respected officers in this facility. She was a twenty-year veteran who could unleash a tongue of acid when appropriate, although she more often spoke words of sweetness from the heart. I admired her genuine qualities.

When I met her that afternoon, she said in a tired voice, "I need to take your class." Ellen and I welcomed her to do so, but she shook her head, telling us, "I have too much paperwork to complete this afternoon."

There were quite a few officers who seemed interested in the classes. Some officers in the recovery unit did the exercises with us while standing at their desks. Officer Natum had just given birth and needed to lose thirty pounds. I gave her an article about yoga postures that sped metabolism, stimulated energy and helped individuals lose weight. She was thrilled to get this information.

I proceeded back to my old classroom and stepped in, happiness surging through my body. It felt so good to be "back home." I started the soft flute music the women so loved on the CD player and pulled the table to the far-left side so we would have room for exercising. I slid the chairs out into the hallway. As I said a silent prayer for guidance and support for these women and the work I would be doing with them, I heard chattering and sounds of laughter coming down the hallway.

First to enter was Luvell.

"What are you doing here?" I asked, surprised to see her again.

Luvell had been released just three months before, and that had been her second incarceration.

She said in a slow, low tone, "Don't you fret. I'm only here for a parole violation. I was working at a Store 24, and they were short of cash. I'm OK, and don't you worry. It will work out for me."

Luvell didn't say whether or not she took the money. It didn't matter what I thought, anyway; the truth was she was back in prison again. I just shook my head, and I think she saw the sadness in my eyes.

A couple of new faces walked in with smiles and friendly greetings. Then I saw Cecily. I felt shocked and disappointed.

"I thought you left," I said.

"I'm back on an OCC," Cecily replied.

"What is an OCC?" I asked.

She explained that there were some discrepancies about her time spent in prison and the calculation of time off for programs.

"It's the fucking system," she said. "I'll be out in a couple of weeks."

Then a woman who I had seen in the recovery unit strutted in to the classroom.

"What's your story?" I asked.

"I wanted to finish my time in the general population unit," Joanna answered.

If the women felt they were finished with their recovery programs, they would sometimes ask to be transferred to GP.

I greeted the women, asked them to sit on the floor comfortably, and introduced myself. I told them about the commitment and the opportunity to earn good time and receive a certificate upon completion of the six weeks. I asked them to introduce themselves, allowing time to express their feelings and whatever else they would like to share with the group.

Luvell, to my left, said she was now in a size twenty dress when she used to be a size fourteen. She then proceeded to do a stand-up routine about being in a Marshall's dressing room, trying to pull down a size fourteen dress.

"The attendant came in and said, 'Dear, you need to go into a bigger size.'

"'I don't need a bigger size. Could you unzip my dress?' I asked.

"The attendant said, 'It is unzipped. You need a bigger size.'

"The attendant left, and I struggled to pull the dress down over my torso, but it reached only my chest. I still have my big boobs from my pregnancy a few months ago. As I kept wiggling and squirming, the attendant comes in with a size eighteen. I was appalled and said to the salesperson, 'Ain't no way this will fit. I know it's too big.'

"'Try it on, dearie, and we'll see.'

"I struggled and squirmed and swung back and forth, trying to get that dress down over my ass, when I think I heard a rip. I stopped and said to the sales lady, 'Let's try a twenty. These designers have different cuts.'

"The salesperson brings in the twenty and said, 'I told you, dearie, you are a twenty and possibly a twenty-two.'

"I put that dress on in a hurry and said in a sassy way, 'Dearie, I am no twenty-two. This twenty is just fine.'"

All the ladies were laughing at Luvell's movements and the voice she used to imitate the saleswoman. I began to feel Luvell wanted to control the class, so I quickly acknowledged what she had said and looked to Kelley and asked, "How are you doing?"

Of all the women I had worked with, I found Luvell to be the most manipulative. As I mentioned earlier, she had several academic degrees, taught at a Boston area college and had a superb singing voice. When she mentioned working at Store 24, I wondered what had happened to her teaching job. She had told me it would be available when she was released. I guess that position had been filled.

PART IV
A New Design

A Different Approach

I had never prepared for class in the normal way, by sitting down and planning out everything I would do. I already had a general feeling about what was working and what wasn't. But the days I went in to the prison, I really listened to my instincts and what they were telling me. So I had been thinking for awhile about trying a new approach and introducing myself to the women in a different way.

On the first day of this new session, my class had been cut down by thirty minutes due to yet another adjustment in the prison schedule. Since I knew in advance that it would be a short class, I brought in some lightweight plastic chairs so we could sit comfortably. When the thirteen women entered the classroom, my instincts told me to go for it.

Once everyone was seated, I said, "Hello," folded my arms across my waist casually and took the big plunge.

"A lot of my friends ask me why I want to work with women in prison," I said. At that moment everyone leaned forward, eyes wide. Some of their mouths dropped slightly open. They were totally silent, intent on what I was going to say, and I continued.

"So I thought about it. And what I realized was that each one of you is a part of me. I may not have been in prison, but there have been times in my life when I felt imprisoned." I said this to connect with them, and then decided to tell them a tiny bit of personal history, as they had so often shared with me. "I've been a single mother, gotten divorced. Now, I'm a grandmother; I'm remarried. I love working here. I have taught this class for two years and hope to continue to do so for a long time."

At the end of my welcome speech, they applauded. It felt like a whole different class from any I'd ever taught before. It wasn't them and me, it was us. I felt so strongly connected to the women from that point on.

I asked them to introduce themselves, sharing a little about their lives. As we moved around the circle, I encouraged them to say only their names, if they didn't feel comfortable revealing more.

The first woman to speak was Erna, an extremely thin black woman, who was in for cocaine addiction and trafficking. Then she said, "I'm a mother of five kids." At this point, she hesitated. Then she closed her eyes and put her hands to her face, gesturing for me to go to the next person. She couldn't speak any more, as she was overcome with emotion.

A woman across the room got up and put her hand on Erna's shoulder and said softly, "It's all right."

I nodded to the next woman to speak.

"I'm only here for two months on a parole violation," Naomi said. "My husband is my biggest supporter. He never misses a visiting day."

When she'd finished, the women said in unison, "Hello, Naomi."

Since they all knew Naomi already, I was a little surprised by the greeting, as though she were a newcomer. It reminded me of an AA meeting.

Louise came next. "I miss my three kids," she said. "They're boys, aged two, seven and ten. They are having a hard time dealing with me being in jail. I have ten months to go." At that point she began to cry. It wasn't just a few tears; she sobbed hard.

"This is the first time I've been able to cry since being in here," she managed to get out. "I've tried so hard to cry, and the tears would never come."

I told her that it was OK to cry.

"When you fill the bucket, you empty it, and then it's ready to be filled again," I said, repeating the words I had learned from my therapist.

Louise nodded her head, agreeing with what I'd said but unable to speak further. Naomi put her arm around Louise; another woman offered a tissue.

Then it was Diane's turn. She had attended my class twice before, when I taught inside the recovery unit. She had spoken about herself only once, to say she was depressed about her father's death. When I led the women in guided meditation, she would leave halfway through it, with tears in her eyes. Later she said that it was just too hard to remember her father.

"I'm an alcoholic, a crack cocaine addict, and I have a gambling addiction," Diane said. "I've been married twice, divorced twice, and I'm gay."

I couldn't believe Diane was talking about things she'd never revealed before, as though it were normal and easy and something she did every day.

"All I have left is my dog, and I'm hoping my family doesn't put her to sleep while I'm in here," Diane added.

Merissa couldn't wait to tell her story. "I'm nineteen years old with a two-year-old daughter my mother is taking care of until I get out in seven months," she told us breathlessly. "I had a boyfriend for the past two years, and I thought he treated me right. But when I got caught with pot in my car and shipped off to jail, he left me cold. I ain't ever heard from him again. He ain't ever going to hear from me."

Tamara, another former student, spoke quickly in her own excitement. "This is my last day! My ten-year-old twin girls and husband and mama are picking me up tomorrow morning." Tamara was beaming like a light bulb as she went on to talk about the receptionist job she would begin the following week and the AA meetings she planned to attend twice a week. She also mentioned joining a gym that teaches yoga.

By this time, all of the inmates knew that it was yoga I was teaching them, but they also understood that they shouldn't use the word "yoga" to describe their class with me. I guess I will never know why prison authorities seemed so suspicious of a practice that has benefited millions of people for centuries; perhaps the male hierarchy thought yoga was a religious cult or that perhaps the women would float out of their cells and away to freedom?

As the women told their stories, I was amazed at how open they were. Most had led similar lives, full of drug and alcohol addictions, and had kids they loved, boyfriends and husbands they yearned for and friends they missed.

Then it was time for the stretching part of class. For fifteen minutes, they stretched in their chairs. For another ten minutes, they listened to a relaxing guided imagery. Then I asked the group to give Tamara some positive words of encouragement for going back into the community. Many of the women brought in the spiritual aspect.

"Believe in God," was a common theme.

At the end of class, Tamara, who had only come to say good-bye to me, hugged and thanked me for my support. I felt honored. As she walked away with the rest of the women, I knew, on a gut level, why I did the work I was doing.

Ellen, the program director, turned to me as we walked to the elevator. "Gee, they really seem to enjoy these classes," she said.

I nodded and smiled. I couldn't really answer. Like Erna and Louise, I was emptying the bucket.

Colors and Numbers

Each female prisoner was color coded and given an ID number. This is how inmates were identified in prison. I began to notice women in red uniforms and soon learned they were called detainees. This meant they were in jail awaiting sentencing or release on bond. Most of the women couldn't post bond, so until their hearing or trial date, they sat in prison. Those women weren't allowed to mingle with other units; if fights occurred it presented a liability, because those women were in limbo status.

Their basic day was spent watching television and drinking coffee. Some of the more enthusiastic women wrote their own pleas and prepared for their court dates. Unfortunately, they were not allowed access to the library, so textbook information was not a privilege. I wondered if they were allowed visitors and how often.

One summer, attendance was low in my program among women in the general population. Ellen decided to include the detainees. Thirteen signed up, and I was enthusiastic as well as curious about this new color group.

They arrived with smiles on their faces and were immediately receptive to my class. I welcomed the change and the new energy of these detainees, because some women from the GP unit made excuses not to attend, telling their friends to tell me they were busy drinking coffee or were not in the mood to exercise. I had become concerned about their lack of enthusiasm, but when I had approached Ellen about the situation, she had simply shrugged her shoulders. I decided not to push for answers. *Just do the program*, I told myself.

I learned that the majority of detainees were in for immigration reasons. Some got caught with no green cards, some had expired green cards, and others were in the country illegally. Anita, an older Haitian woman, shared that she had been in holding for six months and spent most of her time writing her case to present to the judge. She was hoping to go to court the following month. Soya told her sad story. She was a young woman on full scholarship to MIT. She had needed to go back to Iraq for a couple of weeks to help care for her ailing mother. When she returned and got off the plane in Boston, immigration officials immediately transferred her to jail, to await extradition back to Iraq. I was amazed at how many detainees were illegal immigrants.

"She is so beautiful and intelligent but feels helpless and doesn't have a clue what to do," Rosalyn spoke in a saddened voice about Soya.

"She doesn't have enough money to get an immigration attorney," Anita said.

"What about a court-appointed attorney?" I asked.

"Those assholes aren't much good, and it takes a long time to get one. You're better off representing yourself," Suzi piped up.

As I listened to these women week after week, I thought how difficult it must have been to have their lives on hold. Because of the backlog of cases, it could take up to a year to get a court date.

I remembered Sui, who had said when she was sentenced to jail, "This isn't happening to me," and was completely numb and in shock. When they felt the need to share about court, the judges and the attorneys, they often injected humor into their sad tales.

There was Hussie. I didn't know if this name was a nickname or her formal one. She could pull the class into a good laugh when needed. She was anxious to share her adventures, as she called them. I never felt quite sure if she was serious about her antics or just trying to get attention.

"Just wait till you go before a judge and he tells you your sentence in a demeaning voice," Hussie said. "Judge Hitler, I called him, was a real bastard that day; so when he was finished, and I heard his harsh sentence of three years, I pulled up my shirt and said, 'Here's your chocolate for today. Maybe this will sweeten you.' That landed me another thirty days, but it was worth it."

Hearing this story was one of the times when it wasn't easy for me to keep my face expressionless or hide my feelings. I could imagine that scene and wouldn't have wanted to be on either side of the bench that day.

I remembered what Roberta had said, "When I heard my judge sentence me to one year for walking the streets, my first offense, I said under my breath, 'You motherfucker.' When I looked up, he just stared into my eyes with such hate. He was not quite sure what I had whispered. I didn't care if he wanted to add some more time."

She paused, looking agitated. "He made me feel like a piece of shit and didn't buy my story of hookin' to get food for my kids. I swear on my mother's grave, that's the truth," she said in a convincing manner.

I watched as she held her hand over her heart as if she were ready to give testimony.

That day, we were all feeling sad about Molly, who had asked to be transferred to another female prison because more services were available there, and the women got to go outside daily. Molly had been a great one to get the women high on life—always looking on the positive side. We missed her.

As I continued that six-week session, the group size dwindled because of placements and sentencing.

I began to notice some inmates in the cafeteria with orange uniforms. I was curious about them, and I hesitantly asked one of the officers who they were.

"They are in the placement unit," she answered. This meant they had been sentenced and were waiting to be placed either in the recovery unit or the general population unit. They would be set up with programs suited to their abilities and history.

So many colors, so many numbers, and each of them represented a person and where they were in prison life. I wondered if they got excited going from red to orange, or orange to blue or brown. Each color was a step closer to freedom. Did they feel that progression?

The Holding Pattern

It was a perfect summer day, seventy-eight degrees, sun shining, no humidity, as my daughter-in-law, Maura, her two daughters and I drove from Connecticut to New York City for an all-day shopping spree. Although I tried to appear relaxed, I was anxiously awaiting our early evening return, when we would surprise Maura with a fortieth birthday bash. My job was to keep her as far away from the preparations as possible.

Sasha, thirteen, and Katlyn, ten, were snickering and whispering about Mom's reaction and were having a hard time being quiet. They were anxious to see who would be there when we arrived home. They were on the cell phone every hour talking to their father, John, with updates, hiding in the store aisles so as not to be overheard by their mother. John was a natural at sales and marketing and loved organizing parties.

When we were a block away from their home, the girls made one final call, to alert family and friends that it was almost time to greet us.

Maura seemed stunned by the crowd on her front lawn. "Oh my sweet Jesus, what is this?" she asked. The birthday banner, which read HAPPY 40th, swayed in the wind.

Soon, we were greeting family and friends, and I settled in with a glass of wine, tired from the full day's excursion. I was looking around for my grandchildren when my former husband, Brad, walked over.

"I have diabetes," he announced as a greeting.

Why tell me? I wondered. *It's a common disease, and we aren't best buddies.* I waited for what would be coming next, but responded, "You need to follow a strict diet, and leave those desserts alone. Are you seeing a nutritionist?" I asked, not knowing what else to say.

He paused, and put his head down. "I need to talk with you," he said. "Let's go to the garage."

Once inside the garage, he rested his back against the wall.

"What have you told the kids about us?" he blurted out.

A million thoughts skipped through my mind about our divorce, an event that had happened over thirty years earlier. I didn't speak to our children about my past with their father. They didn't want to hear me rehash grievances and remind them of old family memories.

"I … nothing … what are you talking about?" I replied, startled.

"Did you tell them about Syracuse?" he asked, still avoiding eye contact.

I felt chills run through my body. "No," I answered, wondering if a secret from forty years ago had somehow unraveled.

It would have begun with the fact that my third pregnancy had been unexpected, and I had to work full-time at the hospital to support the family. Brad was not employed, and after Adam was born, I went home to stay with my family to recuperate. Brad headed off to Massachusetts where his parents had a second home. He had visions of getting work in that area, using his father's influence.

Still in Pennsylvania with my family seven weeks later, I had insisted he bring the children and me back to Massachusetts. His father paid for the plane fares, and I headed to yet another new beginning. No job had surfaced for Brad. With no X-ray jobs available, I worked the three to eleven shift at the local hospital as a nurse's aide. Brad was left in charge of the three children. I usually came home to a drunken, passed-out husband.

One evening, I had arrived home to find Brad in his usual drunken stupor. After I checked the house and the sleeping children, I began picking up the remains from the evening's dinner and toys scattered throughout the house. I noticed a letter hanging out of Brad's shirt pocket as he slept on the couch. Suspecting feminine penmanship, I slipped it gently out of his pocket and began reading:

Dear Brad,

I miss you, the strength of your body against mine, your hands holding me, promising me everything is going to be OK. I hope we can get together if just for a weekend. Lucy looks just like you. She is so beautiful and bubbly. I wish you were here with us; this is where you belong.

I thought I might faint and reached for the nearest chair. Shocked and crying, I wrote her name and phone number from the letter down, knowing in time that I would contact her.

When I questioned Brad the following morning, he denied that there was a child.

I knew in my heart it was another lie, but I did not pursue the matter further. I pushed the episode away and hid it with all my other shadows, not wanting to face reality. Life continued, full of many turbulent events.

The final motivator for our divorce was a serious car accident Brad had on his way home from a local bar. He had hit a telephone pole, crushing the entire front end of his small compact Chevy, and was rushed to the local hospital. The late-night call came from the nurse in the emergency room. Brad had a compound fracture of his ankle, three broken ribs and a concussion. He was on his way to surgery to have plates and screws put in his ankle.

I thanked the nurse and told her to tell him I'd be in to visit in the morning after I had taken care of the children. Upset and relieved at the same time, I knew this would be my turning point. If he learned his lesson, never drank again, and got professional counseling, we had a chance to save our marriage. Otherwise, that would be it. I was hopeful but hesitant. Two weeks in the hospital and one day home, Brad was out drinking and driving.

That was the final *push*.

Six months later, I divorced him, never looking back.

Shortly after the divorce, I called the phone number in upstate New York—Syracuse, it turned out—and spoke with Tami, his apparent lover. I introduced myself and told her that Brad was a free man. I confronted her about his infidelities and the birth of Lucy, their daughter. She was honest, admitting their affair went on for about fifteen months until we moved back to Massachusetts. Tami and I made tentative plans to get together when I visited upstate New York in the summer, but I decided not to pursue that avenue. She had confirmed my suspicions, and I was free.

My children and I moved back to Pennsylvania, and the secret of Tami and Lucy had remained tucked deep in my trunk of memories. In the midst of this gala birthday celebration, I was forced to open the trunk and confront a shadow of my life I thought had been erased.

"I am going to talk to the boys and tell them about Lucy," Brad said as he began to walk away.

"No, you aren't," I replied harshly. "You'll wait until Catherine comes home from Asia in December and talk to all three together."

"Okay," he mumbled as his wife Sarah approached us.

"He's so worried he's going to lose his kids," Sarah said.

It's not about his feelings, I thought. *Let's be concerned with the children's feelings.* "I think I should be there when he tells them," I replied. "I'm always left to pick up the pieces, and they'll need me there as support."

"I agree," Sarah said. "You should be there."

"I'm not sure he'll allow that to happen," I said, knowing he wouldn't be able to talk freely. He would want to address his issues, his feelings, not mine or those of his children.

Sarah assured me we would have lunch and talk further.

◆   ◆   ◆

Sunday, when I arrived home from Connecticut, my mind buzzed with questions. Not able to focus on anything else, I decided to send Sarah an e-mail.

The most important question for me was Lucy's birth date. It was obvious to me she was born sometime when I was pregnant with my third child, perhaps during the same month when Adam was born.

Did Lucy want to meet my children, her half-brothers and -sister? What was happening in her life? Had she married, did she have her own children? All these questions rose in my mind over and over again.

"We'll do lunch and I'll tell you all then," Sarah replied. Her e-mail left me feeling more frustrated.

My husband listened, but he couldn't, of course, feel the pain as I did. There was no one else I could talk to about the situation. For five weeks, I fed my pent-up emotions with all the goodies I could stuff in my mouth, just like the women in prison. I understood why they tried to fill their emotional gaps with food.

◆   ◆   ◆

Sarah and I finally met.

"When is Lucy's birthday?" I asked anxiously, hoping it wasn't the same date as Adam's.

"I wasn't going to tell you," she answered. "January 4."

I felt numb, but my inner voice spoke, "God works in strange ways." January 4 wasn't Adam's birthday, it was mine, and at the time Lucy was born, I was four months pregnant with my Adam. I wondered if this revelation would affect him more than the other two children. What an insult to me and my children!

Sarah showed me pictures of Lucy and her children and talked about her life in New York.

"She is anxious to meet her siblings and is eager to develop a relationship with our family," Sarah said.

Sadly, Lucy's mother, Tami Nichols, had been killed earlier that year in a car accident, and her husband at the time of Lucy's birth believed Lucy was his child.

This is a time for all to heal, I thought, putting the shadows to rest.

◆   ◆   ◆

I felt like a detainee for the past four months, with a part of my life put on hold. Catherine was in Asia until the beginning of December. I wondered how the holidays would affect all of us.

I couldn't imagine the feeling of being sent to prison and having your whole life put in a holding pattern, waiting for a sentence. How did these women deal with their feelings, just sitting all day waiting for court dates or sentencing? What happened when life could finally move forward?

It was a very difficult time, and every time I saw my children, I wanted to tell them or prepare them, but I couldn't. Then, Catherine would be back in two weeks, and I hoped that a family gathering would take place shortly thereafter. I wanted it to be a time of healing for my children, not another family event where they couldn't express their feelings.

Unfortunately, my presence at this meeting would not be welcomed, so I had to decide how best to prepare them for yet another disappointment from their father. I wished I could believe that he had changed, that he could be more concerned about his children's feelings than his own.

I didn't think my wish was likely to come true. Brad was my revolving door, like I saw with many women in prison, and there appeared to be no permanent resolution: the never-ending saga of divorce, children and family relationships.

The Revolving Door

It was another Monday of exceptionally slow expressway traffic. I was busy doing my usual honking to get drivers out of my way as I moved from the left lane to the middle and back to the left, but none of my maneuvers moved me along as rapidly as I wanted. I did one last double honk and slyly scooted over to the right lane, ready to make a swift exit. I was stressed about running late, a pet peeve of mine, particularly when it came to appointments and meetings. Some of my friends would say I am *anal* in this respect.

I quickly parked my car, signed in and hurried into the cafeteria to greet Ellen and give the heads-up to the program officer to call the units for Fit and Wellness sign-ups.

I rushed to the cabinet to gather my yoga mats and CD player, and then I was off to set up the room for class. As I approached the hallway, I saw the GP women coming up from their unit, either to attend my program or GED studies.

Concentrating on keeping the mats from falling out of my arms, with the CD player gripped in my hand, I looked up for a space to cross the aisle away from the women. Continuing toward my classroom, I saw a familiar face: it belonged to Luvell. This time she was in the GP brown uniform and not in her usual blue one. I froze in my steps.

Before I could say anything she spoke to me. "You have such sadness in your eyes."

"Well, I am sad to see you back here. I would rather it had been outside," I replied in a not-so-compassionate tone. I knew this was one time I couldn't hide my feelings.

"You left with such a positive attitude about caring for baby Annu and reuniting with your daughters, and here you are again," I said, not hiding my disappointment.

"I'll catch you later," she said softly, walking into the cafeteria.

I fumbled as I placed the mats on the floor, still thinking about her re-entry into prison. My thoughts were scattered in too many directions while I prepared for the arrival of the women.

Focusing on my class was a chore, and I felt thankful when it was over. I gathered all my belongings and returned to the cabinet to neatly place the mats on the shelf.

There, at a desk by herself, sat Luvell, with pen and paper and what appeared to be a textbook open. I wondered if she was taking some advanced course for yet another college degree?

Luvell looked up at me and said, "I'm studying for my GED so when I leave here I can get a decent job. No one wants to hire you unless you have a GED or high school diploma."

Before I could respond, she continued, "I know what you are thinking. With the college degrees, the men and family … and I got caught this time writing bad checks so I could eat." She looked down at her hands. "Ain't no one gonna hire you with a prison record, and I was desperate. My life has been lies, and I'm trying to look at who I really am and face the realities of my life as a criminal. Will you pray for me? I know that's all I can say, but I hope soon I can join your class."

I just walked away with a variety of emotions rushing through me, too shocked to speak. I wanted to scream, thinking the sound would relieve my feelings. I desperately needed someone to talk to, so when I saw Minnie, the program officer, I asked if she knew Luvell.

"I don't know her," she said, continuing to read the newspaper.

Briefly, I told Minnie about Luvell and what had just happened, since I was still in disbelief.

Her reply was, "Don't believe any of them. They all lie."

Sadly, I left, still wanting to believe that most of the women I worked with were honest in their tales of home, family and life outside of prison.

As I strolled out of the prison lobby, I thought of the revolving doors in my past and the lessons I had learned. I wondered if this incarceration was Luvell's final stroll through that door.

I walked toward my car, head down, counting the cracks in the sidewalk, careful not to step on them, too drained to cry. I was beginning to look forward to the moment when I would walk into this prison for the last time. My inner voice was saying, "It's time for you to move on."

◆　　◆　　◆

Luvell's story reflects the recidivism that damages not only prisoners but our society. In our enthusiasm for cost cutting, we seem to have lost sight of the necessity to rehabilitate prisoners so there isn't that revolving door. And when adequate programs for the released are not in place, who loses? We all do.

With the "three strikes and you're out" drug conviction, there is no release, and the inmate remains in prison until death. Because of the proliferation of these kinds of laws, the percentage of women in correction facilities has increased to around 8 percent of the prison population. The age range of inmates extends from late teens to the seventies, another reason why prisons are overcrowded.

You, the reader, may wonder what you can do. Are you willing to volunteer your services? Everyone has some form of expertise that could help prisoners. You don't have to be a trained teacher. For example, if you have an interest in music, you could teach prisoners to sing, which is a wonderful way to help them express themselves through sound, which is very healing.

You could, perhaps, help them write, direct, and produce their own plays and explore their latent abilities. You would be amazed at the talent that comes from these women.

Art is another wonderful medium for expressing their emotions. These women harbor rage, fear and anger, which can be expressed through drawing. The benefits of art as therapy have been well documented.

How about helping them to write the stories of their lives? I am sure they could give all of us a few novels that we wouldn't want to put down.

Inquire about aftercare programs for inmates who have been released, and offer your expertise and support when they re-enter the community. Remember, the first twenty-four hours are very important for those coming out into society. What better way for you to work at keeping them from returning to their old habits? There is always something we can contribute to the system in a positive way. Why not make a commitment to do your share so that one day we will live in a world where our prisons are being shut down for lack of prisoners and not because of costs?

Wouldn't it be great if new jobs were created that could employ those leaving correctional facilities? Wouldn't rehabilitation be less expensive and more humane than the revolving door?

Celebration and Commitment

It took years to get minor innovations like yoga mats accepted, but when big changes within the prison system were announced and everyone was scrambling around to find their niche, I thought this might be the opportunity to inquire about having yoga mats to use in our classes.

For a long time, the inmates and I felt frustrated by the fact that I could not get permission to purchase yoga mats that would cushion the cold, hard floor of the classroom. Without mats, we could not do any postures on our knees. Every time I brought up the subject, I met resistance, but I persisted with Ellen to get permission for these much-needed mats. I asked the women to keep requesting mats when back in their unit. One of the women suggested that prison officials were afraid that "there could be contraband in the mats." I couldn't imagine anyone hiding anything useful inside those thin mats.

One day, about two years after Ellen took over as program director, she greeted me in the lobby with open arms and a big smile. "You can buy those yoga mats you've always wanted," she said, obviously delighted to give me good news. After months of asking for the mats, our pleas to Ellen must have gotten through to her.

I quickly headed for Wal-Mart and purchased the mats, which would be stored in a classroom cupboard so that I could have easy access to them.

The women were ecstatic when they walked in the classroom and saw twelve shiny blue mats arranged neatly on the floor, one for each woman. I applauded them for their persistence. "I couldn't have done it without you," I said.

Elice lay down on her mat and shouted, "Now I'm ready to relax!" Susan rolled herself into a ball and rocked back and forth, humming a lullaby. Karen stood on her mat and jumped up and down to see how far her feet would sink into the mat. "Hey, look at my feet. They left imprints in the mat," she said excitedly.

We did lots of postures on our stomachs and even some in the table position. No one complained of sore knees!

◆   ◆   ◆

Ellen had always done her best to accommodate my needs, and I appreciated her help in making my teaching easier. After several years, I had an early-morning teaching time, my yoga mats, and even the freedom to use the word "yoga." I was in high spirits and remembered the ecstatic way Reverend Spence had shouted "Alleluia!" at the prison graduation.

Many mornings when I arrived, Ellen was in the classroom sweeping the floor, moving the chairs out into the hallway and calling the units for the women to be released for my program. I sometimes joked with her, saying, "One must perform all related duties in one's field," explaining that those were the catch-all words that usually appeared in the job descriptions at hospitals where I had worked.

Each week as I placed the mats on the floor for the women, I felt grateful for this important new addition.

◆   ◆   ◆

After several years, my classes began to diminish. Sometimes only two or three women showed up. The word always came back from their papers and from the officers, "they loved your class," but I needed someone to bring their attention to the sign-up sheet in the unit and enthusiastically market my Fit and Wellness program. But who? The women really needed motivation, and I was frustrated that I didn't have the authority to go to the units myself to recruit them.

Only Shawna and Mona, from the recovery unit, showed up for class one day. Charise dropped by to say she wasn't feeling well.

"Those migraines are acting up again," she said as she held her head in her hands. "I need to go back to my cell and rest."

I shook my head and wondered about the other five who had been in class just the previous week. I wasn't in the mood to ask and decided it wasn't worth investigating further. I felt so disgusted with the lack of attendance lately that I was questioning my own reasons for being there.

"We were hoping you'd be here. With all the snow last night, Shawna and I didn't think you'd show," Mona said.

"I know that you look forward to this class, and I honor my commitment to you," I replied in a rather sharp tone. "Look around. There are only two of you today, honoring your own commitment to this class." I felt the need to jump on the soap box.

"Your presence shows me you are ready for positive changes in your life. When you leave here there are many commitments to be made: to yourself, your family and work, to name a few. We all have weak moments, and when those temptations that put you here in the first place reappear, I hope you've learned how to use the tools I've taught you. Breathe, relax, and stretch before jumping into the same old pool of addictions," I said.

As I was giving my sermon, both women were nodding in agreement.

They get it, I thought.

I also pointed out that I felt all programs should be mandatory for every inmate. When I had worked inside the recovery unit, every inmate had to participate in my program.

Shawna spoke up. "Most of them sit all day and gossip about everyone in the unit; who is coming to visit them and how much money their families will bring for their goodies in the canteen. Ain't no wonder they get fatter and lazier."

"I walk by those computers in the hallway," I told them, "and constantly see the women playing computer games, solitaire, hearts and sudoku, when they should be using the computers for something constructive. How do you learn skills to work in the outside world?"

I noticed my voice cracked with frustration.

◆   ◆   ◆

The following Monday I arrived to find my two faithful students along with three new women. Mona and Shawna must have been advertising on their own.

As I began class, Mona asked that I wait a minute, because her mother was coming. My eyes widened, and I blurted out, "Your mother?" I automatically pressed my index finger to my chest as I chanted, "M-O-T-H-E-R."

Nonchalantly, Mona said, "Yes."

In walked a tiny creature who looked like the Mona Lisa, da Vinci's favorite painting. This mother had the same mystical smile that gave the Mona Lisa universal appeal. As she walked past me, her long dark hair flowing, I felt her air of mystery and elegance. She sat on the empty yoga mat next to her daughter. Her blue uniform revealed that, like her daughter, she was in the recovery unit. I began looking for signs that would tell me why she was incarcerated, knowing full well that I probably would not identify any. I searched for some physical or verbal expression that would explain why both mother and daughter were in jail. No clues—only my suppositions.

I had encountered cousins, a husband and wife, but this was my first mother and daughter experience.

◆   ◆   ◆

Mona came into class the following week visibly upset, because her mother wouldn't come.

"She's busy taking a shower," she said. "I tried to talk her into coming, telling her how good it was for her arthritis, but she said the exercises made her tired. She ain't ever going to get better nappin' all day. Just another one of her excuses."

Mona moved toward the window, looked out, and said, "My Jackson is getting paroled today, and his family is having a big bash for him. I sure do wish I could be there. I know this time he's not ever coming back to jail." Mona seemed optimistic.

"Six more months and we'll be married. This being my first marriage, I want that big wedding, the long white gown, a hall filled with flowers, blues music and lots of good food."

She paused as though she were visualizing the scene.

"Jackson said that at our wedding he would sing a song he wrote, called 'Mona's Light.' He says I always have a glow around me that makes him feel first-class."

I was happy to see her thoughts focused away from her mother and on the future, away from jail. Always, I'm left with a sense of mystery about these women. Perhaps one day I'll meet up with one of them, outside of prison, and I'll hear a happy ending.

It appeared that some of the women in prison formed a community with their friends and relatives who were incarcerated with them. When I worked in the hospital, I formed a strong circle of friends, but they were healthy relationships, and we supported each other both at work and in our personal lives. These inmates unfortunately formed the same strong, unhealthy bonds they had formed before coming to prison, and the cycle persisted.

◆   ◆   ◆

I was busy placing the yoga mats on the floor when I saw the shadow of someone standing behind me. It was Johnnie, a wiry gal, who looked to be in her early twenties. I looked up and said, "You're early for class."

"I'm not coming to class today. It's my birthday, but I'll be back next week," she answered in a Caribbean accent.

Are you going to Boston to celebrate? I wanted to ask. *Perhaps a day at the spa? Don't you realize you are in jail?* I had a hard time holding back my thoughts.

Instead I replied, "Why don't you give yourself a special birthday gift by coming to class, and then when you're back in your unit, write down all the things you'll be able to do on your next birthday when you're out of here? That will bring positive support into your life."

Johnnie hesitated, and for a moment I thought I had gotten through to her. But then she shook her head. "No, I need to go back and veg out," she said.

I couldn't decide if "veg out" was different from what she was already doing in her unit.

I guess to some people birthdays signify doing nothing.

◆   ◆   ◆

As I entered the classroom, I saw that Mona, her mother, and Charise were seated on their mats.

"Where's Shawna?" I asked, knowing she wanted to be here, because this was my last class after five years of offering the program.

"She's in the hole for a couple of days. She got word DSS took her kids away from her aunt, and she went ballistic. She was throwing books, chairs and her kids' coloring papers everywhere. Just screamin' and shoutin' those F and S words," Mona said. "The unit guards called for backup, and away she went into the hole."

Didn't my program help her? I felt guilty, sad and disillusioned. Was there possibly something more I could have or should have been teaching? I had no definitive answers.

"It's my birthday!" shouted Charise, changing the mood abruptly. "Are you all going to sing me 'Happy Birthday'?"

We formed a circle around Charise and sang, hugged and chanted, "How old are you now?"

"This is my big fortieth!" Charise raised her arms up and shouted, "Alleluia!" She was proud to be starting a new era.

During class, I watched mother and daughter as they did their yoga postures, side by side, and I hoped this was the beginning of something constructive for both of them.

As I said my farewells to the women, I took Charise aside and thanked her for celebrating her birthday with us. I told her the story of Johnnie who wanted to veg out for her birthday. Charise replied, "This is a perfect opportunity for me to bring in new beginnings. Life begins at forty!" And off she skipped toward her unit.

That's what I'd been working for all these years! *It doesn't end any better than that*, I thought as I waited for the elevator.

A Final Note to the Reader

You may wonder where I'll go from here, after years of working with women in prison. I want to use my experience to launch a new initiative that was inspired by a scene I witnessed at the prison one day.

Officer Bill C. was usually waiting for me at the end of each class when I opened the door, but he was not around that particular day. I walked up to one of the units and asked the officer I saw standing at the desk if he had seen Officer Bill.

"Try the cafeteria," he replied abruptly.

I walked over there but hesitated for a moment, because a group of inmates appeared to be in a study period. They each had books in front of them and were writing quietly.

I spoke from outside the door. "Is Officer Bill C. there?"

A couple of the inmates nodded and called him to come to the door. He waved his hands above his head.

"I'm busy doing the work of several people," he said. "I'm trying to juggle my responsibilities as well as the newly added ones."

He had incurred these additional tasks due to recent cutbacks. He apologized and again waved his hands. "I'm doing the best I can. I'll find you an escort to go back down to the lobby A.S.A.P."

I slowly retreated to the elevator, and an attractive female officer in her early twenties, whose bright blue eyes sparkled as she called my name, was right behind me. *Officer Olsen*, I read on her badge. She greeted me with a smile and stared at the elevator door as we descended to the lobby. She was a new face on this floor. I wondered why she had become an officer. The one thing I had learned was not to ask too many questions. Better to chat casually in a how's-the-weather manner. "Do they silently wonder who I am and what I am about? Perhaps they think I am not really the volunteer that I say I am. Is she working undercover to check the efficiency of the facility?" This was certainly a place immersed in fear, and I needed to take a breath and get a grip.

"Everyone has seemed upright since the recent cutbacks started," I said to Officer Olsen.

"Things are only going to get worse," she answered in an angry tone.

Her words triggered chills through my body. I shuddered to think what that meant!

So many lives are affected when there are big changes, whether it is in large corporations, hospitals or prisons. In hospitals, the patients are affected by cost cutting that reduces the quality of services. In our prison system, cost cutting negatively affects not only rehabilitation programs for prisoners. It also leads to fewer officers, social workers and case workers, which brings additional strain to both staff and inmates.

This reminder from Officer Bill C. and Officer Olsen of the difficult, stressful conditions under which they work has inspired me to continue to consider developing a stress-reduction program for prison officers that would help them retain their compassion and a sense of serenity.

◆　　　◆　　　◆

Recently, I have been speaking to various civic organizations in the Boston area about my role with inmates and my commitment to seeing society work harder toward rehabilitation. I am convinced that we need to create a more positive prison environment for staff and inmates. Some of us have freed ourselves from our own emotional or spiritual imprisonment. Others still need help, so I'll keep working with those who are still imprisoned so that they may find the tools to free themselves.

As Atlanta wrote in her graduation paper: "Ladies, you've touched my soul."

◆   ◆   ◆

My writings reach many people, especially those who attend my meditation and yoga groups, so writing this book has become a valuable tool in my teaching. Writing has also helped me reach a wider audience, like you, the person holding this book in your hands. I continue to learn and heal from experiences both from my work in prison and in the outside world, and I hope you, too, will set yourself free from whatever prison may hold you.

978-0-595-40563-3
0-595-40563-0

Printed in the United States
75586LV00002B/77

9 780595 405633